To Ann & C[illegible] [illegible]son
Alec. Christmas [illegible].

CASTLEBAY, BARRA.

SCOTS FISHERFOLK

BY

PETER F. ANSON

WITH ILLUSTRATIONS BY
THE AUTHOR

PUBLISHED FOR
THE SALTIRE SOCIETY
BY THE
BANFFSHIRE JOURNAL LTD
1950

By the same Author.

THE PILGRIM'S GUIDE TO FRANCISCAN ITALY.
FISHING BOATS AND FISHER FOLK ON THE EAST COAST OF SCOTLAND.
FISHERMEN AND FISHING WAYS.
MARINERS OF BRITTANY.
A PILGRIM ARTIST IN PALESTINE.
THE QUEST OF SOLITUDE.
SIX PILGRIMS' SKETCH BOOKS.
THE CATHOLIC CHURCH IN MODERN SCOTLAND.
THE CARAVAN PILGRIM.
THE SCOTTISH FISHERIES—ARE THEY DOOMED?
THE BENEDICTINES OF CALDEY.
HOW TO DRAW SHIPS.
BRITISH SEA FISHERMEN.
HARBOUR HEAD—MARITIME MEMORIES.
A ROVING RECLUSE—MORE MEMORIES.
THE SEA APOSTOLATE IN IRELAND.
THE APOSTLESHIP OF THE SEA IN ENGLAND AND WALES.
THE CHURCH AND THE SAILOR.
CHURCHES—THEIR PLAN AND FURNISHING.
THE RELIGIOUS ORDERS AND CONGREGATIONS OF GREAT BRITAIN AND IRELAND.

TO

ALEX. JOHN McKAY

CONTENTS

Page.

Introduction.

Chapter.

I. Scottish Sea Fisheries in the Past 1

II. The Social Background of the Fisher Folk 12

III. Religion and Superstitions 28

IV. The East Coast 52

V. Orkneys and Shetlands 59

VI. The West Coast—Mainland and Islands ... 63

VII. Methods of Fishing—Trawling, Drift Net, Inshore, etc. 70

VIII. Fishing Vessels—Old and New 100

Maps 114

Comparative Statistical Tables for 1938 and 1948 123

Bibliography 158

Details of Old Types of Scottish Fishing Vessels 160

Index 164

List of Illustrations

Castlebay, Barra .... *Frontispiece*

Page

Macduff—Drifters and Seine Net Boats ... Facing 1

Peterhead .... Facing 12

Eyemouth Fishermen (1890) 17

Aberdeen Fishermen (1880) 19

Fraserburgh Drifter Crew (1930) 20

Fisherman and Fish-Wife 22

Baiting Lines at Auchmithie 25

Fraserburgh .... Facing 28

Drifters at Buckie .... Facing 52

Wick .... Facing 57

Mallaig .... Facing 63

Trawlers at Aberdeen .... Facing 70

Hauling-in A Trawl Net 71

Hauling Drift-Nets 79

Landing Herring at Lerwick 85

Inshore Fishing Boats, Port Seton 92

"Zulu" Fishing Boat .... Facing 100

Shetland "Fourareen" 101

Shetland "Sixern" 102

"Skaffie" 104

"Fifie" 105

Loch Fyne Boats 107

"Lass o' Doune" (Macduff, 1949) 110

Introduction

My object in writing this book has been to record the customs, traditions and social background and the daily life of a particular class of men and women who have played an important part in the evolution of this country. It must not be regarded as a serious treatise on the fishing industry in Scotland. For I am mainly interested in fishermen, fishing ports and fishing vessels from the point of view of a marine artist. My memories of brown-sailed Scottish "Fifie" and "Zulu" fishing craft go back more than half a century. For nearly thirty years I have been drawing and painting Scottish fishing boats of more recent types. For the past twelve years my home has been beside the harbour of a busy fishing port on the Moray Firth, but I have visited every other fishing district of Scotland again and again during the past quarter of a century. As a fisherman remarked to me not so long ago: "There's mair fishermen ken Peter Anson, than Peter kens them!" I certainly feel that they have now adopted me as a member of a very large family. Just because of this sense of intimacy it is not always easy to write about them objectively.

The sea fisheries are of much greater importance in Scotland than in England and Wales. Until recently they employed seven times as many men in proportion to population as in those countries. The fishing industry is spread all round our indented coastline. The alarming decay of the sea fisheries which has gone on since the first world war may yet involve the disappearance of countless self-contained communities which have lived by the sea for generations, and their absorbtion into the population of towns and cities. Fewer and fewer sons of fishermen are following in their fathers' footsteps. Their parents realise that sea fishing has now become a far too risky means of earning a living. No matter how strongly a lad may feel the call of the sea, he is often discouraged from taking up fishing as a career.

Successive Governments have attempted to carry out numerous schemes to restore our fisheries to their former state of prosperity, but the outlook at the moment is not too hopeful. It is a problem much too complex for almost any set of economic experts to solve. The most alarming feature about most of these schemes is that they suggest that the only solution would be what amounts to little less than the "nationalisation" of fishermen; reducing them to the status of miners, transport workers and other classes of the community. From the point of view of politicians what is wrong with Scottish fishermen is that they are far too individualistic: they object to being tied up in red tape and having their freedom of action curtailed! They have always been a race of men characterised by a spirit of independence and hardihood. Hitherto they have largely failed to work together on any sort of co-operative basis. They have never succeeded in putting up a united front. So what will be their future? Will the remnant that is left have to follow the example of English fishermen and become the virtual slaves of big companies and combines? Will they be classified as a species of "Civil Servant" and work for the State? Is it yet possible to find an alternative and give our fishermen a chance to earn an adequate livelihood while preserving their independence?

Such matters are really outside my sphere, and I can offer no solution for these intricate problems. It is difficult to convey a true idea of the present condition of our fishing industry or to generalise about it, for it is in a perpetual state of flux. It might be summed up by saying that there is still more than enough fish in the sea, except where the shoals have been depleted by over-fishing, but too many fishermen and fishing boats in comparison with the means of marketing the fish which is landed. Nature is prodigal in its generosity, but man seems incapable of making proper use of these gifts! A comparison of the statistical tables given in the appendices will show how every Fishing District or port in Scotland has progressed or declined in the past ten years. These have been taken from the Reports of the former Fishery Board for Scotland and the present Fisheries Division of the Scottish Home Department.

My thanks are due to the following persons—and many others—for information, advice and criticisms: Messrs R.

Stuart Bruce (Whalsay Island, Shetland), George Clark (Edinburgh), R. Callum Morrison (Bernera), John M. D. Smith (Montrose), Andrew Lyall (Macduff), Alex. J. M'Kay (Macduff), George Smith (Macduff), James Smith (Buckpool), W. Winchester (Macduff), and the Rev. G. W. Baird (Kirkmichael). The serialisation of most of the chapters in *The Banffshire Journal* has given me the opportunity to correct many mistakes pointed out by its readers.

The statistical information has been published with the permission of the Fisheries Division of the Scottish Home Department.

PETER F. ANSON.

Harbour Head,
Macduff,
Banffshire,

October 1949.

MACDUFF—DRIFTERS AND SEINE-NET BOATS.

CHAPTER I.

SCOTTISH FISHERIES IN THE PAST.

FISH have played an important part in the religious, social, and political history of Scotland from a very remote period. On the arms of Glasgow is still depicted the salmon with the ring in its mouth, recording the miracle reputed to have been performed by St Mungo in the sixth century. Salmon fisheries were bound up with the Church throughout the Middle Ages. This valuable fish had been caught and preserved long before the first charter was drawn up. making over certain salmon fisheries to a monastery. They belonged to the Crown. Many abbeys and other religious houses were granted rights of fishing by the Kings of Scotland. The Valliscaulian priories of Pluscarden, Beauly and Ardchattan derived a large part of their incomes from salmon fisheries from their foundation early in the thirteenth century. About the same period, cured salmon was being exported to England from Aberdeen. But there does not seem to have been enough fish caught in Scotland to supply the needs of the inhabitants, especially in Lent. In 1304 it was necessary to appeal to Newcastle for salt haddocks and cod to feed the King and his court while they were staying at St Andrews. The royal party were also given 'porpoys' and lamphreys, the latter imported from France.

Herring were caught in the Firth of Forth, even more on the Firth of Clyde. Most of them were dried and exported. In 1299-1300 red herring are mentioned among the king's stores at Berwick.

The white fisheries were controlled by the Law of the Four Burghs, and were strictly burghal monopolies. Each burgh had the powers to pass regulations affecting the price, quality and sale of fish. The building of boats and harbours, also wood for barrels, and the provision of salt—all these and much else connected with the fisheries were controlled by the burgesses.

By the middle of the fourteenth century, Dutch, Flemish and German vessels were regularly engaged in fishing off our coasts. During the following century, they became such a menace that the parliament of James III enacted that "great ships, busses, pink-boats, with nets, and all other necessaries of fishing" should be found. In 1493 James IV. ordered that all coastal burghs were to build vessels of twenty tons to be employed in fishing, and that "stark idill men" were to be pressed into service as crews. Nevertheless foreigners gained a supremacy over the North Sea herring fisheries. They established themselves in Shetland, where many merchants from Hamburg, Bremen and Holland had their headquarters. It was only on the Firth of Clyde that there was any big fishery carried on by Scotsmen.

By the middle of the sixteenth century it was a common sight to behold as many as two thousand Dutch herring "busses" assembled in the Shetlands. Later on in the year they sailed south and carried on fishing off the coasts of Aberdeenshire and Fife. James V., in a vain effort to deal with the situation, tried to start colonies of fishermen in the Hebrides, where the Dutch had long established themselves. He encouraged families from the coast of Fife to emigrate to Lewis. But the islanders drove them away, preferring the Hollanders to the Fifers.

It was Charles I. who created the first of the many Royal Fishing Companies to compete with the Dutch herring fishermen, and to fit out busses for that purpose. None of them managed to prosper. The first society, known as the '*Association for the Fishing*' was established in 1632. Great enthusiasm was shown for the object, but the actual performance seems to have been insignificant. One of the chief obstacles was the constant friction between the English and Scots who formed the council. James VI. in 1609 made the first attempt to wrest the herring fisheries from the Dutch. He issued a proclamation which forbade foreigners to fish off the coasts of Scotland and England unless a licence had been obtained—in London for the English waters, in Edinburgh for Scotland. The Dutch protested, and long diplomatic negotiations resulted. A further tax on Dutch fishing vessels was made in 1617, paid at first, but afterwards refused. The Dutch fishing fleets were protected by armed convoys, and carried on in defiance of the law.

'*The Association for the Fishing*' collapsed in 1640. Another attempt was made about this time, to start a fishing colony in Lewis, but once again it was a failure, owing to the antagonism of the natives and to mismanagement of affairs.

On the West Coast of Scotland, the herring fishery had been carried on with small open boats from time immemorial. Most of the catch was cured and sold to France and Spain. James III. made regulations, by which each boat paid a certain quantity of fish to the Crown, which formed part of the hereditary revenue. The inshore herring fisheries on the Firth of Clyde was controlled by the 'merchant adventurers' of Glasgow, Greenock, Dumbarton, the Isle of Bute, and Ayrshire. Curing yards and warehouses were built at Greenock in the reign of Charles II., but purchased by the Town Council of Glasgow in 1684, who continued to carry on the Clyde fisheries with considerable profit. The boats used were quite small, each with a crew of four men, and provided with twenty-four nets. As many as nine hundred were sometimes employed during the season, which lasted from July 25 to Christmas. In 1674 some 20,400 barrels of cured herring were sent to La Rochelle. The Clyde fisheries were badly hit with the passing of the Act of Union in 1707.

'*The Society of Free British Fisheries,*' founded in 1750, was the last of the royal fishing companies. Two busses were built on the Thames, and two Danish skippers and twelve Danish seamen engaged as part of the crews. The following year, two more busses were fitted out, and fishing was carried on in Shetland and off the Hebrides. After a chequered and unprofitable existence, the Society finally collapsed in 1772, proving that it was almost impossible to compete with the Dutch in an industry of which they had the experience and control for many centuries. It was not until Holland ceased to be quite such an important maritime nation that Scotland began to benefit by its own herring fisheries.

With the failure of the last of the Royal Companies, it was left to the Clyde merchants to carry on the herring fisheries with busses; the number of which had increased from two in 1751 to 261 in 1766. The number of busses declined for some years owing to foreign wars and domestic difficulties, but rose again to 153 in 1783.

On the East Coast, the herring seems to have been regarded of little commercial value until the middle of the 18th century. Even as late as 1767 the Caithness fishermen merely caught it with iron hooks to use as bait for white fishing. But that same year, three Caithness merchants fitted out two sloops, nets and gear at their own expense, and fished for herring with great success in the Moray Firth. This seems to have been the first definite attempt on the east coast of Scotland to adopt the methods of the Dutch—at least for more than a century. The experiment was repeated for the following season, and with such good results, that other merchants fitted out sloops, and Wick soon became the chief centre of the herring fisheries on the east coast.

An important date in the history of Scottish fisheries is 1718 when George I. gave his assent to an Act of Parliament by which fishermen were to be rewarded for their catch by a bounty. Bounties were paid for various kinds of fish, e.g. for every barrel of white herring of thirty-two gallons, exported beyond the seas, the bounty was 2s 8d; for full red herrings, 1s 9d per barrel; for empty red herrings, 1s per barrel. The building of fishing vessels was also rewarded by a bounty. For the first time regulations were laid down as to fishing seasons. The Bounty system, which was modified from time to time by successive Acts of Parliament, continued in force for over a century. It was finally abolished in 1829. It did not benefit the West Coast fishermen until 1787.

There can be little doubt that the gradual change which took place in the condition of the Scottish fisheries was due in the first instance to the *'British Society to extend the Fisheries, and improve the Sea Coast of the Kingdom,'* founded in 1786 by a number of influential Scotsmen, with the Duke of Argyll as president. They learned by the failures of the previous Royal Fishing Societies of the past century, and set to work in a very different manner. Their chief object was to erect fishing villages or stations on the mainland and islands, by which the poverty and distress of the inhabitants could be relieved. A sum of £40,000 was subscribed privately. Land was bought at Wick, Ullapool, and Tobermory, where houses, wharves, and curing establishments were built. The district of Wick, known as Pultneytown, was erected in 1808, and named after the then president of the Society. The excellent work which it initiated without any government support, has been ignored by many modern writers on the fishing industry, and it deserves better recognition, especially by Scotsmen, for it was this definitely national organisation which did more than anything else to "improve the sea coast of the kingdom" and to extend the fisheries—which were its definite objects.

Full details of the Scottish fishing industry at the time of the foundation of the British Society can be found in the Parliamentary Reports which were issued between 1785 and 1805. They give intimate details, not only of the economic state of the fisheries, but also of the conditions of the fisherfolk themselves, their methods of work and their life ashore. Taken as a whole the impression one gains is that the fisheries of Scotland were in a very backward state at this period, particularly in the Highlands. The lairds gave little or no encouragement to the crofter-fishermen. In many instances we read that they even forbade them to cure their fish above high water mark, and it was almost impossible to obtain stores of salt or barrels. The crofters themselves were generally far too poor to spend any money on such articles, so they had to content themselves with drying fish for their own consumption.

The Napoleonic wars had a disasterous effect on our fisheries, owing to the closing down of foreign markets for cured herring. Quite the most exhaustive account of the fishing industry in this country at the close of the 18th century is to be found in John Knox's book published in 1789, whose full title is '*A View of the British Empire, more especially Scotland, with some proposals for the improvement of that country, the extension of its fisheries, and of the relief of the people.*' Knox informs us in his preface, that "having in 1764 been led through curiosity to view the rude magnificence of the Highlands of Scotland," his attention was soon attracted by "the less pleasing scenes of human misery in all its shapes; unalleviated by the cheering rays of hope, or of any of the comforts which the lower ranks of mankind, inhabiting richer soils, enjoy in a certain degree." He discovered that a "great body of people, and those the most virtuous of our island, were dragging out a wretched existence, perishing through want, or forced through wild despair, to abandon their country, their kindred, and friends, and to embark, moneyless and unknown, the indented slaves to unremitting toil and drudgery, in boundless deserts, at the distance of 3,000 miles."

John Knox seems to have been so roused by what he saw in all parts of Scotland, particularly on the coasts, that he resolved to write this book; a bulky volume of over six hundred pages, as full of data and statistics as any modern government Blue Book. One is tempted to make quotations from its pages, but space forbids, and one must be content with saying that the general impression gained by the writer is that the Scottish fisheries were in a very bad way, and that it was high time that the Government did something definite to relieve the appalling conditions of the unfortunate inhabitants on the coast and islands of Scotland. The same impression is obtained after reading the even more detailed Parliamentary Reports already mentioned, which were issued between 1785 and 1805, and whose writers could hardly be suspected of any undue bias in favour of "North Britain" and its people.

Both on the east and west coast, the fisheries were at a low ebb. There were endless complications connected with the working of the Bounty System. Foreign trade was at a standstill, and on the east coast especially, great distress was often occasioned by the irregularity of the appearance of the herring shoals at this period, a natural phenomenon which no legislation could deal with. Some years the herring would forsake the coast altogether and remain in deep waters, out of sight of land. The boats then in use were too small to venture after them, so the stock of salt and barrels which had been laid in would be unused. Knox suggests that when a herring shoal has been detected at sea, it should be "notified to the inhabitants by the town bell, and expresses sent in writing, and signed by the magistrates, to all the adjacent towns on the coast."

Among the many interesting bits of information which one learns from the bulky tomes of the 1785-1805 *Reports of the Committees on British Fisheries,* is that there were 797 small boats engaged in the herring fisheries on the west coast of Scotland in 1797. In the Shetlands, the herring fishermen were said to be in great poverty, and it was hoped that the Government might purchase the three existing stations. The North Sea fisheries were dismissed as "not worthy of the attention of the public." It was pointed out that they would remain in this condition until large decked vessels could be built in place of the small open boats which were quite useless except inshore. Indeed it was only the

Western or Hebridean fisheries which were regarded seriously in these Reports. But it shows that the inhabitants of the islands derived little direct benefit from it, and all the profit went to the "merchant adventurers" on the Clyde who controlled the Western fisheries.

Hindrances to the development of the West Highland fisheries existed in the difficulty of obtaining stores of barrels and salt. There were also the disadvantages of the crofter system, by which the same person was both farmer and fisherman. The poverty stricken condition of the people as a whole, together with the unseaworthy character of their small boats, affected the fishing industry.

Many proposals and suggestions are made in the appendices on the Reports as to how the Scottish fisheries could be improved. They include the abolition of the heavy tax on salt; a drastic revision of the Bounty System, and the control of all fisheries by the Government. It is interesting to note that in spite of the frequent demand for larger decked boats, there were many witnesses who in their evidence, maintained that small undecked boats were more suitable and more economical for the herring fisheries—the same argument being brought up again nearly a century later, when the big "Zulus" and "Fifies" were first built.

Between 1787 and 1797 there were 2949 vessels fitted out for the herring fisheries in Scotland, with 33,666 men, as compared with 55 vessels and 701 men in England. Practically all of these busses and sloops were owned by the merchant adventurers on the Clyde.

Adam Smith in his '*Inquiry into the Nature and Causes of the Wealth of Nations*,' first issued in 1776 has much to say about the Bounty System, of which he strongly disapproved. A more recent authority on the sea fisheries—Dr W. T. Jenkins—argues that however unsound the Bounty System may have been from the standpoint of political economy, there can be no doubt that it greatly helped in developing the herring fisheries during the 18th century.

The heavy duties on salt were not abolished until many years later, in fact, they were increased after 1801, and no real improvement in the conditions of our fishermen took place until 1808, when the Bounty System was revised, and much more detailed instructions given as to the lawful methods and times of fishing for herring, without the observance of which the bounties could not be obtained.

This legislation remained in force until 1829, when the Bounty System was finally abolished. During these twenty-one years, the herring fisheries developed rapidly, especially on the east coast. Gutting and curing establishments were opened at the following ports—Fraserburgh (1810), Helmsdale (1813), Macduff, Banff, Portsoy, and Cullen (all in 1815), Lossiemouth (1819), Burghead (1817), Peterhead (1820), Lybster (1830). Further south, the older ports of Dunbar, Eyemouth, Burntisland, Buckhaven, and Cellardyke, made similar progress, and on the west coast the Loch Fyne herring fisheries developed.

The 1830 Report states that "an increased means of employment and an ample supply of wholesome food have been found to the labouring classes; fishing villages have been erected, harbours built, and extensive curing premises raised in the most complete style, and agriculture has benefited and waste land reclaimed by the use of the offal of the fish as manure, arising from the practice of gutting having become general in consequence of the bounty being confined to gutted fish alone."

The boats increased in size during this period to an average of 15 to 20 tons, and whereas formerly 60 to 80 crans of fish had been reckoned as a good fishing for each boat in a season, by 1830 the fishermen were not content with less than an average of 200 crans for each boat.

Ice was first used in connection with the fish trade about 1780 for packing salmon. About 1794, fresh herring were packed in ice at Dunbar and sent to London by fast sailing vessels. It was not until the middle of the 19th century that ice was imported from Norway.

The result of the series of Parliamentary commissions into the state of the British fisheries which were carried on between 1785 and 1805, led to the appointment in 1808 of a Board of Trustees to direct and control the industry. In 1815 they were formed into a Board of Commissioners for British Fisheries, which appointed a secretary, general inspector, and some thirty or forty officers at the various fishing centres, whose chief work was to deal with the payment of bounties. But when the Bounty System was finally abolished in 1829, their duties were confined to the branding of herring. Scotland had to wait until 1882 until it was given a Fishery Board of its own. It took the place of the "*Commissioners for the British White Herring Fishing*"—by which name the original body, formed in 1808, had been known for many years.

In 1893, the Board opened a laboratory at Dunbar which was transferred to Torry, Aberdeen, in 1900. It had control of all the practical administration of the fishing industry round our coasts. Its staff included, administrative, clerical, marine superintendents, inspectors, and thirty-two fishery officers. Several fishery vessels were maintained for scientific purposes and patrolling the coasts. Between 1882 and 1938, about sixteen Acts of Parliament were passed dealing directly or indirectly with Scotland's sea fisheries. In some ways Scotland was more fortunate than England, since it did have its own independent Fishery Board, whereas it was a department of the Ministry of Agriculture and Fisheries that looked after the industry south of the Borders! At the present time, our fisheries are directed by officials of the Scottish Home Department, whose headquarters are at St Andrew's House, Edinburgh. They maintain the services formerly carried on by the Fishery Board.

Throughout the nineteenth century, the Scottish fisheries, particularly the herring fisheries went ahead. The export trade in cured herring developed on a scale never dreamed of. Fortunes were made and lost. There were good years and bad years. The white fish export trade prospered too, until the electrically-dried white fish of Norway finally destroyed the sun-dried fish of Shetland in Spanish, Italian and Portuguese markets. Then with the dawn of a new century, came signs that this prosperity might not last for ever.

The decline of the Scottish fisheries which started after the first World-War is best shown by these figures which cover the years until two years before the outbreak of World-War Two.

Total number of fishermen.

1913	32,678
1937	19,327

Other persons dependent on the fishing industry.

1913	52,448
1937	35,063

Grand Totals.

1913	85,126
1937	54,390

Fishing vessels.

1913	8,534
1937	5,217

Amount of fish landed by British and Foreign vessels in Scottish ports.

1913	7,828,350 cwt.
1937	4,853,793 cwt.

It is also interesting to compare the amounts of fish landed in other countries of Northern Europe between 1913 and 1936. The total amounts are calculated in 1000 tons.

	1913.	1936.
Scotland	397.6	257.3
England	820.5	804.4
Germany	181.4	569.0
Norway	731.5	1146.9
France	193.2	575.3
Iceland	92.2	261.0
Holland	147.1	160.4
Sweden	72.8	110.1
Denmark	64.4	83.6
Faroes	22.4	44.0

To what is this catastrophic decline due? Why was it that eight out of ten countries should have made such big advances in their fishing industry within twenty-three years, and England and Scotland fallen behind—Scotland worse than any of them?

The reasons cannot be entirely economic, for some of these countries were then without a twentieth part of the resources of England and Scotland. In Norway, the number of fishermen rose from 63,000 in 1913 to 120,000 in 1936. In this same period, the number of fishing vessels had increased from 59,000 open boats and 7,000 decked boats to 63,000 and 12,000 respectively. There were 17,650 fishermen in Denmark in 1913 and 18,887 in 1936. There was an almost equal increase in Sweden. The advance in Iceland and the Faröes was even more remarkable.

By 1929 matters had reached a crisis. The British Government set up a Committee "to inquire into a report upon the condition of the fishing industry, etc." An exhaustive Report was published in 1932. Three years later the Herring Industry Act was passed and a Herring Board established. Other Reports were issued dealing with the White Fisheries, and led to the passing of the Sea Fish Industry Act of 1938.

This Parliamentary legislation provided for the new marketing schemes, and much else. It looked as if something was being done on practical lines for our fishermen, but with the outbreak of war in 1939, hopes were dashed to the ground. About 10,000 Scottish fishermen out of a total of approximately 17,000 served in the Royal Navy and Merchant Navy during the second world-war. The Admiralty took over 671 Scots fishing vessels.

CHAPTER II.

THE SOCIAL BACKGROUND OF THE FISHER FOLK.

In order to understand the social background of present day Scottish sea fishermen, it is essential to have some idea of the conditions in which they lived and worked during the past. They have always formed communities of their own, more conservative in many ways than agricultural or industrial workers. They were and still are more closely knit together. Until comparatively recent times they intermarried amongst themselves. It was a rare thing for a young man to take a bride from a neighbouring village, and an almost unforgiveable offence if she came from the country. Until the close of the last century, most fishermen's sons followed in their father's footsteps and went to sea as a matter of course.

The life of the average fishermen about the middle of the nineteenth century was even more laborious than it is to-day. Until about 1850 few of the boats were decked, or even half-decked. The crews were exposed to wind, rain and sea. Earnings were precarious in the days of sail, especially during the herring season, for the shoals of fish often vanished for weeks on end, and there was then no means of locating them. When the crews had to depend on sail or oars for catching this perishable species of fish. even more so, bringing it back to port, life was a gamble at the best of times.

This is how the daily life of the average Scottish fisherman a hundred years ago is pictured by James Thomson in *The Scottish Fisheries*, published in 1849.

> "Perhaps in the world generally it is not thought of how constant and intermitting the toil of the Scottish fishermen is, particularly during the eight weeks of the herring season. In every seven nights they are but two in bed, on the Saturday and Sunday. During the other five, they may have a little slumber, for an hour or two in the middle of the day; this is from the time the nets are sent into the fields to dry, till when they have again to be collected and carried to the boat. The unquiet and restless closing of the eye, induced by fatigue, in a moment of rest at the fishing ground, partakes but

PETERHEAD.

little of the good of nature's sweet restorative—the bare bank of the boat, the couch—the canopy of heaven, for covering.

"When the herring fishing is over, and the fisherman with his family is returned to his own habitation, he has to set out for the mussel ground for the winter's bait; this accomplished, the hook and line is got in order for the haddock. In this fishing there is more rest than in that of the herring, yet the cold and wintry weather of November has to be encountered.

"In the spring cod and line fishing, there is again a longer absence from their home. The open boat forms again the lodging for the night. For as this latter fishing is carried on at a distance from the land, and assumes the character of the deep sea, there would seem to be matter for just opinion that greater comfort and greater protection should be afforded. If a decked sloop, of 20 tons and upwards, is to be fitted out, here is the fitting use. Additional safety would thus, and undoubtedly be given to the voyage of several days, and there is as little question that the sources of the fishing would be improved." (Pp. 176-77.)

A century ago the curing of dried cod on the East Coast was mostly done by the fishermen themselves. Towards the end of the summer when the cure was completed, they generally went south with the fish; bringing home some of "the more bulky necessaries of life, such as coals, etc. In this manner they have the whole of what their industry in this fishing may produce." (Op. cit. p. 180.)

* * * * * * *

The typical fisherman's house in almost every town and village on the East Coast of Scotland was usually planned on definitely functional lines until quite recent times. However, local authorities since the first world-war, seem to forget that houses should be designed to suit the traditional way of living of those who are to occupy them. Most Scottish fishermen, at least those who engage in herring fishing, still own their nets and gear. They need lofts or sheds in which to store them. Very few modern houses provide either. All the fishermen can do is to store their nets and gear elsewhere, and to pay to have their nets mended. There is no place where this can be done at home as in the old days.

A hundred and fifty years ago, a fisherman's house on the coast of Fife may have been little better than a low, narrow smoke-grimed "but an' ben," but it was definitely a *home*. The walls were rough and often unplastered. The roof bore the marks of axe and adze. The floor of the kitchen was bare earth. Beneath the open fireplace stood the "creepie," a low stool which served as a chair. Under the little deep-set window, filled with coarse greenish glass, through which the sun dimly found its way as through a thick curtain, stood a strongly made kist or sea-chest, holding clothes. The big double-bed was hidden in a recess, closed-in either by doors or curtains. The furniture of the living room was completed by a table, press and a corner shelf, with its array of dishes and ornaments brought home by seafaring sons. Two other rooms on the same level provided accommodation for the invariably large family. In the yard outside were tarred sheds for storing nets and gear. Then, as to-day, a fisherman's house was never complete without its clothes lines.

It might be said that it was almost invariable to find one storied fishermen's houses on the east coast of Scotland until comparatively recent times. About 1810, the magistrates of Aberdeen decided to erect new houses for fisher folk in Footdee. Plans for two-storied houses were prepared. But the fisher families flatly refused to consider living upstairs. They insisted on earth floors as being more healthy. The first objection may have been due to prejudice. Actually an earth floor, at least in the kitchen, was far more practical for a room where lines were baited. The writer in the *New Statistical Account* tells us that the fisher houses in Footdee were clean and comfortable. Thirty years later, James Bertram noticed that "the Houses of Footdee are peculiarly constructed. There are neither doors nor windows in the outer walls, although those look to all the points of the compass; and none live within the square but the fishermen and their families, so that they are completely isolated and secluded from public gaze as a regiment of soldiers within the dead walls of a barrack." He goes on to tell us that the total population of the two squares—which are still standing to-day—was 584, giving about nine persons for each of these two-roomed houses. "In the South

Square," he writes, "only three of the houses are occupied by single families, and in the North Square only three, the others being occupied by at least two families each—one room apiece—and *four* single rooms in North Street contain *two* families each. There are thirty-six married couples and nineteen widows in the twenty-eight houses, and the number of distinct families is fifty-four."

Here is another contemporary picture of fisher life in Footdee during the sixties of the last century: "The interior of the houses is as clean, sweet and wholesome as could well be desired. Their white-washed walls and ceilings, their well-rubbed furniture, clean bedding, and freshly-sanded floors, present a picture of tidiness such as is seldom met with among classes of the population reckoned higher in the social scale." . . . Ask any employer of labour where he gets his best apprentices, and he will tell you that for industry and integrity, he finds no lads who surpass those from the fisher-square of "Fittie," as it is locally called.

A century ago, the typical fisher house at Buckie and elsewhere on the Moray Firth coast, consisted of two or three rooms, with a lean-to shed for the nets. Most of the houses by that date were roofed with red tiles or slates. The older ones were still thatched with turf. During those prosperous years of the herring industry before the first world war, a new type of fisherman's house was evolved on much more elaborate lines. They are to be found in almost every town and village from Peterhead to Nairn—strongly built houses that suggest affluence and thrift. Many of the exteriors have carved quoins, lintels and finials, either of granite or freestone. The interior woodwork is usually varnished pitchpine. In some of the larger houses—one might almost term them mansions—there are stained glass windows half-way up the stair, with owner's steam-drifter depicted on the centre pane. The two sitting-rooms are filled with the best furniture that money could buy. The kitchens are immaculately clean, and fitted with the latest labour-saving gadgets. But what is so interesting is the functional planning of these houses. *They were designed for fishermen.* Part or the whole of the upper floor is given over to a spacious loft for storing gear and mending herring nets. Very often the loft is approached by an outside staircase to avoid bringing nets, etc., into the house. Until about fifteen or twenty years ago, smaller houses suited to the needs of less prosperous fisher families were still being erected in many of the East Coast ports. All the living rooms were still on the ground floor, and upstairs was the inevitable loft. But with the craze for standardisation which has swept over this country, the modern fisherman has to be content with just the same type of house that would do for a baker, a butcher or any labouring man. What's more, he is only too thankful to get any sort of house for himself and his family—even a "pre-fab."! His home is no longer the expression of himself or his calling.

It would be a complete mistake if any reader of this book formed the impression that the average Scottish fisher family on the East Coast lives in poverty or squalor. It is usually very much the opposite. In some towns and villages, there are well-to-do fishermen who own motor cars and who have erected garages next to their houses. Admitting that there are differences in the scale of living, yet generally it is on a far higher level than that of the land-worker, either in the town or in the country, even in these times when fishing is most precarious.

* * * * * * *

There was a great diversity in the clothes worn by fishermen during the last century. Fashions varied according to districts. For instance, about 1850 every fisherman and fisher lad at Eyemouth wore a pair of loose-fitting blue serge breeches, tied at the knee with tapes. Over these were drawn a thick pair of long woollen stockings reaching well over the knees. On shore the cumbersome leather sea-boots were replaced by slippers. The every-day "rig" of the Eyemouth fisherman of half a century ago (and earlier) comprised a hand-knitted jersey, and blue bonnet, complete with tassel. At one time, a very tall "lum hat" was worn, tilted at the back. It was known as a "rakie step." Cheese-cutter straw hats, with glazed tops, and little round seal-skin caps became popular in after years.

Henry Farnie, in his *Handbook of the Fifeshire Coast* (p. 187), describes the Cellardyke "cadgers" about 1840, galloping away with their cart-loads of fish; "their blue bonnets pulled belligerently down the nape of their necks--ready for anything, from selling a herring to engaging in a single combat with a customer who is inclined to haggle a little about the price."

EYEMOUTH FISHERMEN (1890).

In the late sixties of the last century, the fisher lads of Footdee in Aberdeen wore moleskin trousers, so James Bertram tells us in *The Harvest of the Sea.** At Ardersier, near Inverness, the women were "remarkable for the peculiar brevity of their lower garments." *New Statistical Account,* Vol. XIV., p. 472.

A hundred years ago it was a common sight at Wick, and elsewhere on the East Coast, to find the fishermen putting to sea dressed in "nor-wester fearnaught jackets," and high leather boots, reaching to the knees, with kit on their backs, containing food and drink for the night.

Standardisation in all ways of living, even more so "Clothing Coupons," during and after the second World-

*The great shipyards of Aberdeen were at Footdee (Hall Russell's and Alexander Hall's). The shipwrights of those days always wore moleskins, hence the fisherlads of "Fittie" found moleskins ready to hand in the Aberdeen shops. Moleskin trousers were practically the standard wear of shipwrights in Buckie and elsewhere on the Moray Firth up to about 1904, but they were never worn at sea.

War, have affected the fisher fashions, both male and female. A quarter of a century ago, it was easy to determine to what district a fisherman belonged by the way in which his jersey was knitted, each had one or more favourite patterns. Even to-day Scottish jerseys differ from those worn by English fishermen. They are much shorter, and fit tightly round the body and neck. There are usually two buttons on the neck. Until dark indigo-blue wool got scarce during the second world-war, it was rare to find jerseys of any other colour, except among the "Hielenmen," who often sported gayer colours, similar to those of Harris tweeds. To-day fishermen, both on the East and West coasts wear jerseys of any colour, according to what wool can be bought. The dappled-grey Faröe wool is becoming increasingly popular for thick jerseys.* To protect the jersey, a loose-fitting brown linen jumper, known as a "slop," is still worn at sea, or when engaged in dirty jobs ashore.

It is now very rare to find a fisherman wearing the old-fashioned sleeved waistcoat.† Trousers, made with a flap, are also obsolete.‡ Dark brown or indigo blue pilot-cloth trousers, with cross pockets, were until recently, almost an unofficial uniform all along the East Coast. But everywhere dungarees and overalls are becoming more common. A man has to take greater care of his trousers than he used to do! Within living memory, all seaboots were made of strong leather. These have been superseded by black or white rubber boots. Very often the once universal bright yellow oilskin "frocks" have given place to similar garments of black mackintosh.‖ When at sea, trawlermen usually wear heavy white duffle trousers. Berets of all colours of the rainbow are popular with trawler crews. At one time, not so long ago, all drifter skippers

---

*The loose-fitting, thick, light-coloured jersey was originally worn only by trawlermen.

†The sleeved waistcoat was more of a "go ashore" garment.

‡Blue jerseys, leather sea-boots, and heavy kersey or pilot-cloth trousers with flaps were always worn for working among herring nets with their fine mesh. Exposed buttons would be a nuisance and even dangerous to a fisherman during his work.

‖An oilskin jacket, sou'-wester, and oilskin trousers reaching just below the knees were worn by most East Coast fishermen before they adopted the oilskin "frock" from England. It was maintained that the former garb was less awkward when hauling or shooting nets.

wore soft felt hats when at sea.* These have now been discarded in favour of "bonnets."

For funerals, a navy blue suit, white shirt, black tie and a bowler hat are still *de rigueur*. Formerly, on a Sunday, a fisherman was content to don his best jersey, which had never been washed. To-day, more often than not, he would not venture far from his house without a collar and tie.

* * * * * * *

James Bertram (*op. cit.* 429) gives us a picture of Newhaven as it existed about eighty years ago.

"Up the narrow closes, redolent of bark, we see hanging on the outside stairs, the paraphernalia of the fishermen —his "properties," as the actor would call them : bladders, lines, and oilskin unmentionables, with dozens of pairs of particularly blue stockings that seem to be the universal

ABERDEEN FISHERMEN (1880).

wear of both mothers and maidens. On the stair itself, if it be seasonable weather, the wife and the daughters, repairing the nets and baiting the lines—gossiping of course with the neighbours, who are engaged in a precisely similar pursuit ; and to-day, as half a century ago, the fishermen sit by their hauled-up boats in their white trousers and their Guernsey-shirts, smoking their short pipes, while their wives and

---

*This custom seems to have been adopted from East Anglian skippers, and did not last for many years.

daughters are so employed, seeming to have no idea of anything in the shape of labour being a duty of theirs when ashore. In the flowing gutter, which trickles down the centre of the old village, we have the young idea developing itself in plenty of noise, and adding another layer to the

FRASERBURGH DRIFTER CREW (1930).

incrustation of dirt which seems to be the sole business of these children to collect on their bodies. The juvenile fisher folk have already learned from the mudlarks of the Thames, the practice of sporting on the sands before the hotel windows in the expectation of being rewarded with a few halfpence. 'What's the use of a skin for siller before they've got their dinner?', we once heard one of these precocious youths say to another who was proposing to solicit a bawbee from a party of strangers."

A vivid and detailed impression of the fisher folk at Buckie at the close of the eighteenth century has been recorded by the Rev. George Donaldson in the *Old Statistical Account* (Vol. XIII., p. 422). He describes them as sober, frugal and industrious, peaceable and friendly to neighbours; decent and exemplary in their attendance at the ordinances of religion." He refers to their taste for comfortable houses, and implies that they are, on the whole, well clothed and well fed, and decently lodged. "No moral duty is seldomer violated by them than chastity. They go to sea as boys, at fourteen years of age, become men at eighteen, and marry soon after . . . . always the daughters of fishers from eighteen to twenty-four at the most."

Mr Donaldson goes on to relate that, "the fisher wives live a most laborious life. They assist in dragging the boats on the beach, and in launching them. They sometimes, in frosty weather, and at unseasonable hours, carry their husbands on board, and ashore again, to keep them dry. They receive the fish from the boats, carry them fresh, or, after salting, to their customers, and to market, at the distance, sometimes of many miles, through bad roads, and in a stormy season. When northerly winds, or a high sea, prevent the boats from going a-fishing, the men are employed at repairing their sails, mending their lines, or making new ones. It is the province of the women to bait the lines; collect furze, heath, or the gleaning of the mosses, which, in surprising quantity, they carry home in their creels for fuel, to make the scanty stock of peats and turfs prepared in summer, last till the returning season."

* * * * * * *

The Scottish "fishwife" has managed to achieve a world-wide fame, largely because of the song *"Caller Herrin'."* When George IV. visited Edinburgh, he is said to have declared that the Newhaven fishwives were the handsomest women he had ever beheld. Their ordinary costume a century or more ago consisted of a white "mutch" or kerchief, tied round the head, stout navy-blue bodice and kilted skirt, beneath which appeared a striped blue and white petticoat, black shoes and stockings. White stockings were only for gala dress. A shawl was crossed over the bodice. Its sleeves were tucked up as far as the elbow. Over the shoulders was worn a blue serge cloak. Around the neck was suspended the wicker creel by means of a leather strap. With the weight on her shoulders the woman hawked her fish through the streets of Edinburgh. The Sunday costume was more elaborate. James Bertram, writing in 1869, tells us that the Newhaven fishwife "is always supposed to ask double or treble what she will take. On occasions of bargaining, she is sure, in allusion to the hazardous nature of the guidman's occupation, to tell her customers that 'fish are nae fish th' day, they're just men's lives.' The style of haggling she adopts when dealing with the fisherfolk, if attempted in other kinds of commerce, gives rise to the well-known Scottish reproach of 'D'ye tak' me for a fishwife?' "*

FISHERMAN AND FISH-WIFE WITH BASKETS.

The wives of Fisherrow, now merged into Musselburgh, were formerly quite as famous as those of Newhaven. From early childhood they were accustomed to gather bait, and bait lines. Two or three days a week they made the journey

*Harvest of the Sea. P. 426.

to Edinburgh on foot, carrying a heavy load of fish on their backs. Should the boats be late in landing their catches, it was not unusual for the women to perform their journey by relays, three women carrying one basket, and shifting it to the other every hundred yards or so. Sometimes they did the five mile journey in less than an hour. All that matters was to get the fish to Edinburgh in time for dinner.

The story is told that on one occasion three Fisherrow women covered the twenty-seven miles between Dunbar and Edinburgh and back in five hours. This in itself is a proof that these amazons had the strength of men. Their amusements were masculine. They played golf long before it became the fashionable diversion of ladies. On Shrove Tuesday, there took place a football match between the married and unmarried Fisherrow women. It was the former who were generally the winners. The rude eloquence of the Fisherrow fish-wifes was famous, but according to the parish minister of Inveresk, writing in the *Old Statistical Account*, "their licentiousness in speech is not accompanied by licentiousness in morals." Indeed they were a hardy race. It was no uncommon thing for a woman to give birth to a child, and to be carrying a heavy creel of fish into Edinburgh three days later. They never wore shoes or stockings except on Sundays. They were usually devoted wives and mothers of large families.

During the latter part of the eighteenth century, the Aberdeen fishwives worked just as hard as did those of Newhaven and Fisherrow. John Knox in his *View of the British Empire, more especially Scotland* (p. 503), writes that "great quantities of fish are brought to town from the villages to the south and north, even as far as Newburgh, fifteen English miles distant, upon women's backs in baskets, with a breast rope fixed to them. These poor drudges will thus travel fifteen miles before breakfast, with a heavy load upon their backs; and such is the force of habit, that they would think it a punishment to be obliged to return home without a load in their baskets equal in weight to a third of their outward-bound cargo. If they have neither goods nor provisions to carry home, they generally take in ballast of stones, and thus they trudge homeward with four shillings in their pockets, the produce of the fish; which, if purchased from fishermen, produces a clear profit of one shilling."

At Footdee, Aberdeen, the women ruled the men. Not only did they bait the lines, carry the fish to market and sell it, but they kept hold of the money. The men had nothing to do but catch fish. James Bertram, writing about 1869, informs us that "there are many fishermen in Footdee who will not go to sea as long as they imagine their wives have got a penny left from the last hawking excursion. The women enslave the men to their will, and keep them enchained under petticoat government."

In his description of the parish of Boyndie in the *New Statistical Account*, the Rev. A. Anderson gives us many interesting details concerning the fishwives at Whitehills, Banffshire, about a century ago. We learn that the woman is "allowed an influence which in any other condition of life would appear little consistent with either feminine propriety or domestic order. She usually claims the entire proceeds of the white fishing, which lasts ten months of the year, as her exclusive prerogative, and in addition to baiting her husband's lines, she prepares fish for sale and hawks it round the country."

No matter the locality, the story is always the same—the amazing strength and terrific capacity for work on the part of the women of the fishing towns and villages. It is not only in Buckie where contemporary writers of the middle of the last century refer to the women and girls as "handsome, goodlooking; and the very picture of health." The same facts are commented on at Avoch (Ross-shire), Dunbar, and Ardersier, near Inverness. In this last-named village the women chewed tobacco at all times when not working, a habit which is not mentioned in accounts of other fishing communities at this date, although it may have been common about a century ago.*

* * * * * * *

The Scottish tradition that the fishing industry concerned women just as much as men persisted until recent times. As has been stated already, in the old days when line fishing was the principal occupation of the towns and villages on the East Coast, the women found more than

*On most parts of the East Coast the older fisherwomen smoked the "clay cuttie," and chewed a "blade or two" until fairly recently.

enough to do at home in baiting lines, collecting bait, and selling fish. Each line had more than one thousand hooks to be baited, and this was always looked upon as an essentially feminine occupation. With the expansion of the herring fisheries towards the end of the last century, it became common for women and girls to leave their own districts

BAITING LINES AT AUCHMITHIE.

every summer. They found employment in gutting, salting and packing herring, not only in Scotland, but also in ports on the east coast of England. So it was quite a normal thing to find a woman or girl leaving home in June, and to remain in Shetland, Wick or in the Outer Hebrides or some other stations on the mainland of the Highlands until August. She would then pack up her "kist" and move to Fraserburgh or perhaps the Isle of Man. By the end of September she travelled south to Yarmouth or Lowestoft, where she lived in lodgings until the late autumn. For the rest of the year, she stayed at home, where she found plenty to do in mending nets before starting out again on her annual tour the following summer. The result of all this moving around the coasts of Britain was that the typical Scottish female fish-worker acquired a self-assurance and knowledge of the outside world that was rare in a woman of another sphere.

It was a hard life in many ways. It involved long hours of standing over open troughs, exposed to wind and rain and cold. The foul brine in which the herring was soaked, made even small cuts difficult to heal. The girls' hands were often a mass of sores and wounds. When there was a big shot of herring they had to work overtime. There was little leisure for rest or meals. Nevertheless most of the women—young and old—enjoyed this roving life. In Stornoway, Yarmouth and Lowestoft they were usually fairly comfortable in lodgings, but at Lerwick, Stronsay and in many other ports they lived in huts with few of the ordinary conveniences of civilisation, until Government intervention forced the curers to provide better accommodation for their female workers.

Times have changed, but even to-day, women and girls still find employment in the herring industry, but not on such a scale as before the last war. In bygone years, hundreds of girls came over from Donegal in Ireland and found work in the herring ports. The majority of these female workers belonged to east coast towns and villages, but many were drawn from the West Highlands, especially some of the islands of the Outer Hebrides.

Except at Lerwick, where the lassies lived in huts close to the piers and wharves, and could see the drifters coming in, it was necessary for them to be summoned from their lodgings by boys. In a few minutes they would be hurrying down the street, or being driven to the curing yards on a lorry—a cheery, happy-go-lucky crowd of girls, dressed in long waterproof aprons, seaboots coming fell up over their knees, shawls pinned over their shoulders above woollen jerseys, their hair covered with a handkerchief, fastened tight over their head. Round their fingers were bound bits of rag to prevent them being cut or pierced with herring bones.

Only the older women still go about with black shawls covering their heads. Twenty-five years ago few fishermen's wives ever possessed a hat. If they did they only wore them when away from home. The modern fisher-lassie, when she is at work usually wears dungarees or slacks. Her legs, once hidden beneath a mountain of petticoats and aprons, are now displayed for all to gaze on! What's more she powders her face, plucks her eyebrows, uses lip-stick, and has her hair 'permed.' She is not ashamed to be seen striding down the street with a cigarette in her mouth. When off work it would seem that the ambition of many a Scottish female fishworker of to-day is to achieve something of the glamour of her favourite film star!

No doubt it was due to this close intercourse of men and women in the Scottish fisheries that helped to preserve their national characteristics.* Where a whole family takes its part in the catching, curing and selling of fish, and where everyone has a share in the job, it is quite a different thing to the conditions found in those big centres of the trawling industry in England. In Scotland, every man, boy, woman and girl retained a sense of individual responsibility, so long as the fishing industry maintained its freedom from combines and company ownership. With the threat of "Nationalisation," this big family spirit is almost certain to disappear for ever. Granted that there were many abuses in the old system, yet it was founded on the basis of the family, burgh or village—i.e. on the "community." If these essential elements of healthy life are destroyed then, it is difficult to prophesy what lies ahead.

---

*In some districts, including Buckie, it is still the custom for women to give the drifters a thorough wash-out and cleaning before they leave port for the herring fishings.

CHAPTER III.

RELIGION AND SUPERSTITIONS.

Fisher folk in almost every part of the globe are much more conscious of an invisible world than the average landsmen. They either fear their "gods" and propitiate them, or defy them. Before the Reformation, the Scottish peasantry, taken as a whole, had drifted into a state of ignorance of the fundamental doctrines and practices of the Catholic religion. Calvinism does not seem to have succeeded in uprooting the superstitions, many of them pagan in origin, that were part and parcel of daily life among the less educated class of Scots. During the eighteenth century, superstition "grew up side by side with the most austere belief of orthodox religion, like flowers and weeds springing up in an ill-kept garden. Each was held with equal tenacity in the same mind, unconscious of any incongruity. Trust in charms, omens, incantations, were rife amongst them all. . . . . Those notions and these practices were guarded from the Kirk, and were kept as furtively as the teraphim by ancient Jews, who worshipped them in private and adored Jehovah in public. Mostly deeply rooted were superstitions among the peasantry in remote districts separated by moor, and hill, and loch from contact with towns—regions where schoolmasters were scarce and kirks were powerless. But in fact there was no place where they were not prevalent . . . . side by side with belief in the doctrine of the Confession of Faith was the respect for notions whose sources were pagan, or popish or satanic."* To understand the character of bygone generations of Scottish fisherfolk, and even those of the present time, it is worth while studying some of these rites, unknown to the Kirk, which played such part in daily life from birth to death.

* * * * * * *

On the birth of a child in a fisherman's family, it was common for a fir-candle or a basket containing bread and cheese to be placed on the bed to keep the fairies at a dis-

---

*H. G. Graham. *The Social Life of Scotland in the 18th Century.* P. 190.

FRASERBURGH.

tance. A pair of trousers hung at the foot of the bed was reputed to have the same effect.* A strict watch was kept over the mother and child until the former had been "kirked," lest the bairn should be wafted away by fairies.

Before a boy was looked upon as a full-fledged fisherman, it was usual for him to undergo an initiation ceremony, which took various forms. On parts of the West Coast, the lad was seized by his fellow boatsman and dipped in the sea, or in a nearby loch, to initiate him into his craft.† At Eyemouth there was a much more brutal ceremony. The boat's crew assembled in one of the many public-houses. The boy was placed with his back against the wall. Immediately above him hung a rope with a noose from a block and tackle. The rope was passed round the lad's neck. Close to him was a salted roll and a jug of beer. He was ordered to eat the roll. If he hesitated, one of the men tightened the noose by pulling the rope. As the boy tried to eat the salt roll, the skipper threw beer over his face. Another man sprinkled his legs, while two more repeated the words "weather" and "lea." The beer symbolised the spray of the "weather" wave on the bow of the boat; also the water sweeping over its deck—both of which the fisher-lad would soon experience at sea. Very often verses, such as the following were sung or said, intended as a lesson in fisher morality:

From St. Abb's Head tae Flambrough Head,
Whan'er ye cut, be sure ye bend,
Na'er lea a man wi' a loose end.

Boys often had to be captured by force before they would submit to such initiation, or "brothering." Once it was over they were treated as grown-up men.‡

It would be impossible to mention all the superstitions connected with marriage. There were countless ways to find out who was to be the husband or wife. Some of the rites or incantations could be performed at any time, others only only on certain days. For instance, the young women of

---

*W. Gregor. *Notes on the Folk-lore of the North-East of Scotland.* P. 5.

†Carmichael. *Carmina Gadelica.* Vol. IV, p. 36.

‡D. M'Iver. *An Old-Time Fishing Town, Eyemouth.* P. 197. Should a shipwright-apprentice cut himself for the first time with his "each" (adze), his journeyman mates would say, jokingly, "You are brothered noo."

Fraserburgh used the following method of divination at Hallowe'en. They set out for the adjacent village of Broadsea, now absorbed into Fraserburgh, and drew a straw from the thatch of one of the houses, the older the thatch the better. The straw was taken to a woman in Fraserburgh, famed for her second-sight. She broke it, and if events were to go right with the maiden, she drew from the broken straw a hair of the same colour as that of the young man the girl hoped to marry.*

In the North-East of Scotland there was a firm belief in love charms right on until the last century. A potion made of orchid roots was regarded as most effective to arouse love. The "loons" and "quines" of the fishing villages carried on their love-affairs by night.

At a late hour the young man set out for the abode of his lady-love. By the time he arrived all the family had retired to rest. He tapped at the window. The happy maiden,

"Wha kens the meaning o' the same,"

was quickly at the door, undid the bar, and admitted her lover. If he could not be admitted by the door, the window was lifted, and he made his entrance by it.†

* * * * * *

Marriages were usually arranged by the pair without the knowledge of their parents, although in some cases everything was done in a much more business-like manner. Fishermen married very young. About a century ago the minister of Boddam stated that most of the lads in this village married between the ages of eighteen and twenty. The same custom existed almost everywhere on the East Coast. There was a saying that "no man can be a fisher and lack [want] a wife." This was true. Most of the work connected with the fishing was done by women and girls. It was they who gathered the bait, prepared it, baited the lines, cured the fish, and sold it. A wife was an economic necessity to a fisherman, not a luxury!

Fisher weddings in olden times were great events. The so-called "Penny Weddings" involved the contribution of a

---

*Gregor. *op. cit.* P. 86.
†Gregor. *op. cit.* P. 87.

certain sum by every guest. In some places, several weddings would take place on the same day, usually a Thursday or Saturday. The festivities were kept up for two or three days and nights. In villages round Aberdeen, it was the custom for the two youngest members of a boat's crew to carry a large flag into the house, wrap the bride in it, and give her a kiss.

Part of the bride's trousseau at Rosehearty and elsewhere, usually consisted of a kist. This was always the first piece of furniture to be moved from her parents' house to her new home. It was never locked until it was outside the door. It had to be carried so that it never touched the ground. It was then put on a cart and locked. At Macduff, a fisherman never locked his kist when leaving for the summer herring fishing until it was outside the house.* There was a superstition that a bride's trousseau should never be taken away on a Saturday. On one occasion this seems to have been forgotten at Crovie. It got as far as Gardenstown, and for fear of bad luck, had to be put in a boat and taken back to Crovie.

At Newhaven, where old traditions lingered on until comparatively recent times, the marriages were celebrated with great expense. For some days before the ceremony took place, the bride went round the village in full dress, accompanied by her bridesmaids. The purpose was to invite friends and relatives to the wedding. The costume of the fishermen consisted of loose-fitting white trousers, velvet waistcoats, and blue jackets with brass buttons. On the wedding day the men went to the bridegroom's house, and marched with him to the kirk or manse. After the wedding, all assembled in the hotel for a great banquet. This continued throughout the night until the afternoon of the following day.

We learn from the *Old Statistical Account* that during the latter years of the eighteenth century, the brides of Buckhaven in Fife wore a richly ornamented girdle or belt. It was laid aside and given to the next bride deemed worthy of wearing it. At Collieston, Aberdeenshire, the fisher weddings were marked by great hilarity. After a substantial banquet, all the guests made their way to the links at the end of Forvie Sands, to the music of a fiddle. Here they

---

*W. Gregor, *Folk-lore Journal*. Vol. II, p. 353.

danced the famous "Lang Reel o' Collieston." It was a *long* reel in every sense. A writer in the *Banffshire Journal* describes the scene about eighty years ago. "To see the lang reel danced on the greensward under the blue canopy of heaven on a sweet afternoon in summer, is a treat worth going many miles to enjoy. Not only would the eye enjoy a rare feast, but what with the sweet music of the violin, the merry song of the lark in mid-heaven right overhead, the ringing guffaws of the juvenile spectators, the clapping of hands, and the loud *hoochs* and *whoops* of the dancing fishermen, all commingling and co-mingled with the murmur of the billows breaking among the rocks, the ear would have a banquet of non-ordinary kind nor of every-day occurrence."

A hundred years ago at Buckie, the kirk session used to exact a pledge of half a guinea before a fisherman's wedding that no rioting or fighting would take place. If too much whisky was drunk, and brawling or even bloodshed were the result, the money was handed over to the poor. If the guests remained sober, the pledge was returned to the bridegroom the following Sunday.*

After the "Penny Weddings" at Ardersier, near Inverness, the bride would visit her neighbours who were bound to make her a substantial present, usually a piece of furniture. This practice was called "thigging." In many places on the North-East coast it was the custom for the wives and mothers of members of the crew to which a bridegroom belonged, to present each other with a basin of flour on the day of a wedding. When a newly-married wife went to live in another village, the night before her departure, friends would turn up with gifts of fish, flour and domestic utensils.†

The Rev. Walter Gregor tells us that "on an evening shortly before the marriage day, or on the evening before the marriage, the bride and bridegroom set out in company, often hand in hand, to invite the guests. The bridegroom

---

*It was a common marriage custom in Buckie and the adjacent villages for the bride and bridegroom to invite the guests by personal calls. The older folks were also invited to what was called the "beuking": i.e. a supper which was held on an evening before the wedding when the presents were on view, and of course presents were given to them also.

†W. Gregor. *Notes on the Folk-Lore of the North-East of Scotland.* P. 100.

carries a piece of chalk, and, if he finds the door of any of his friends' houses shut, he makes a cross on it with his chalk. This mark is understood as an invitation to the marriage. A common form of words in giving the invitation is: "Ye ken faht's adee the morn at twal o'clock. Come ower, an' fess a' yir oose wi' ye," or "Come ane, come athegeehir." The number of guests is usually large, ranging from forty to a hundred or a hundred and twenty."

"On the morning of the marriage day, the bride, after being decked in bridal array, goes the round of her own friends in company with her 'best maid,' and repeats the invitation to such as she wishes to be of her party. The bridegroom, accompanied by his 'best man,' does the same, and repeats his invitation to those he wishes to be of his party."*

Sometimes the wedding took place in the kirk, at other times in a house. Before entering the kirk or house the "best man" had to put down the heel of the bride's shoe; the bridegroom doing the same with his own shoe. It was a common custom, after the wedding ceremony was ended, for the whole party to make the circuit of the village. When the bride entered her future home, a towel or napkin, and a dish filled with bread were offered her by female friends. The towel was spread over her head, and the bread was poured over her. Then, in many places it was usual for her to make up the fire on the hearth.

Marriages at Crovie generally took place on a Saturday. The bridegroom did not go to sea the following week. The bride's *plinisan* or trousseau, comprising a kist, full of clothes, and a bed, and other pieces of furniture, was never taken home on a Friday, for this was considered most unlucky. So the transport was generally effected on the previous Thursday. In Gardenstown there was a superstition that the bridal bed must be made up by a woman giving suck, "having milk in her breasts," otherwise the bride would have no family. In this same village it was a custom for the bridegroom to take off a stocking before getting into bed, and throw it among the bystanders. The one who caught the stocking would be the first to be married. At Boddam the bride did not go to her own house until the

---

op cit. Pp. 97-98.

night after the wedding. She spent the marriage night in her father's house.*

After a fisherman's wedding on the North-East coast friends made presents. In some villages, the wives and mothers of other members of the crew to which the bridegroom belonged, offered basins filled with oatmeal. Elsewhere they gave dried fish, or anything needed for the new home. The bride entertained her guests to tea, and sometimes whisky was drunk.†

* * * * * * *

The home life of the old-time Scottish fisherman was bound up with traditions and superstitions, the origin of which is often obscure. At Buckie and in other places on the Moray Firth coast fishermen used to go down to the beach on New Year's Day, fill a small flagon with salt water, pick up some seaweed, and take them home. The salt water was sprinkled over the house, and the seaweed put above the door, on the hearth and roof beams.‡ To spit on the hearth was regarded as a sure way to bring luck at sea. It was unlucky for a man to give another a light from his pipe. However, if salt was thrown into the fire it was supposed to break the spell.|| It was unlucky to burn fish-bones or shells of bait.¶

On the Banffshire and Morayshire coasts, fishermen used to be scared of "ill-fitted" persons, i.e. people with an "evil foot." Should one of these unfortunate people enter a house where nets or lines were being made, they had to be destroyed, unless somebody could be found to lay the spell cast by the "ill-fitted" visitor. At St. Combs, near Fraserburgh, it was the custom to lock the door when baiting lines, lest any unlucky person should try to enter. To avert any chance of bad luck, the lines were passed round

---

*Gregor. *op. cit.* P. 100.

†*op. cit.* P. 101.

‡G. Hutcheson. *Days of Yore.* P. 42.

||W. Gregor. *Further reports on the Folk-Lore in Scotland.* P. 458.
Ask a match from a fisherman, more likely than not he will give you one with a little bit broken off, in case he loses his luck!

¶W. Gregor. *Folk-Lore Journal.* Vol. III, p. 146; Vol. IV, p. 16.

"Bile me, fry me,
But dinna burn my banes,
Or I'll lie scarce
On your hearth stane."

the hearty before being taken out of the house.* Should any visitor call while baiting was going on, he or she was generally asked to sit down and bait one or two hooks. What is curious is that this seems to have been the only occasion when it was permissible to wish "good luck" to the fishing.†

At Boddam, Aberdeenshire, when lines were baited for the first time after a fisherman's wedding, it was the custom to begin with one hook, then turn the "scull" or flat basket upside down, draw the lines across the floor, put them back again in the scull, and start the work again.‡ It was very unlucky if anybody counted the nets, or walked over them. It was even worse if this was done by anybody with certain physical peculiarities.

When a new boat was to be built, it is curious to find that Friday was regarded as a lucky day for the keel to be laid down.|| Some shipwrights were convinced that they knew if a boat would be lucky by the feel of the first blow of an axe on the wood of the keel.¶

Certain days were looked upon as being more propitious than others, and these varied according to the locality. Once a new boat was in the water, whisky and bread were distributed to all present. The boat was then named. A bottle of whisky was broken over the stem and stern.§ In certain ports on the North-East coast, the skipper's wife, on

---

*Sébillot. *Folk-Lore des Pécheurs.* P. 84.

†Gregor. *Folk-Lore Journal.* Vol. III, p. 191.

‡W. Gregor. *Revue des traditions populaires.* Vol. IV, p. 663.

||W. Gregor. *Folk-Lore Journal.* Vol. III, p 180.
But not all builders and owners regarded Friday as likely to bring bad luck to a boat if launched on that day—the tide may have been considered more important to the less superstitious!

¶The story is related that in some boat-yards when a new boat was to be built, the owner might hint to the builder to remember to place a gold sovereign in a recess in the keel (in the stem onset joint) for luck to the new craft. The builder kept his secret, just where he placed the coin, and said nothing about it.

§When a boat "was at her height," i.e. fully planked, she was "damped." This meant that the shipwrights were treated to refreshments —lemonade, beer, and perhaps whisky, with bread and cake.
When the boat was launched, a banquet in the builder's loft or shed was provided by the owners. The boat, the builders and owners were toasted in turn. A new boat was turned with the sun when afloat after launching.
It was not uncommon for an owner to come into a yard, asking for "the captain himself." When asked what was to be done, he would say, "Just a sma' jobbie to gie the boat a clinkie." The boat had not been successful, so this might change her luck.

the arrival of a new boat, took corn or barley meal and sprinkled it over the vessel.* It is significant that the minister of the parish was never asked to bless a new boat. Ministers—unlike Catholic priests—were regarded as bringers of bad luck to the fishing. Very often a horseshoe was nailed to some part of the boat, usually to the mast. A new boat was generally allowed to leave the harbour or shore the first time the fleet put to sea after its arrival. On its return from the fishing grounds, the owner's wife gave bread and cheese to the crews of all the vessels that arrived after it.† At one time fishermen in the parts of the Outer-Hebrides used to send on ahead one of the crew to make sure that no women were about when they were putting to sea.‡ It was a common belief that if a woman stepped over a fishing-line no fish would be taken with it.||

Cats were far from popular, at least when met on the way to a boat. In some fishing villages there was a saying after bad luck had been encountered: "We must have met a cat this morning."¶ On the other hand in Shetland it was said to be lucky if a cat runs before a fisherman, but the reverse if it crosses the road.

Rabbits, hares and foxes were dreaded even more than cats on the East Coast of Scotland.§ Pigs were the most dangerous of all—it is almost a risk to mention them in writing!** To hear the mooing of cows when nets were being shot was looked upon as a bad omen by some fishermen.†† In some of the Aberdeenshire villages, it was believed that certain actions were enough to bewitch a boat—for instance, to walk round it in a particular way.‡‡

It was looked upon as more than an insult to ask a fisherman, on proceeding to sea, where he was going. He would be almost certain that some disaster would befall him, or that he would catch no fish that day. Sometimes he would answer: "De'il cut oot yer ill tongue!" Should it be necessary to refer to a kirk, for churches were often used as landmarks, the word "bell-hoose" was substituted. The

*Gregor. *Folk-Lore of the North-East of Scotland.* P. 197.
†Gregor. *op. cit.* P. 198.
‡Bassett. *Legends of the Sea.* P. 427.
||*Folk-Lore Journal.* Vol. I, p. 355.
¶*Folk-Lore Journal.* Vol. III, p. 309.
§*Folk-Lore Journal.* Vol. II, p. 200.
**Pigs were sometimes called "grumphies."
††Sébillot. *Folk-Lore des pécheurs.* P. 189.
‡‡*Revue des traditions populaires.* Vol. IV, p. 660.

minister was described as "the man wi' the black quyte." Some people were regarded as gifted with the power of taking away fish with the evil-eye. Of such and such a persons, it would be said, "he glowrt the fish oot o' the boatie." The spell could be removed by making a noose or "bicht" on the halyards and passing the boat through it—over the bow, and under the keel. On the shore it was sure to bring bad luck to point with the finger to boats at sea. But it was quite safe to point with the whole hand.* It was looked upon as just as risky to count boats when at sea. In many villages on the Moray Firth coast it was—and still is—common to borrow an article of trifling value from a neighbour before a boat left home for another fishing station, but with the intention of not returning it. The luck went with what was borrowed.†

It was supposed to bring bad luck to a new boat to put in ballast removed from an old boat. Care was taken to include among the ballast certain red and white stones, supposed to possess magical properties.‡ If a boat was wrecked and lives were lost, no fisherman of the port to which she belonged would dare set foot on her, neither would any of the inhabitants risk breaking her up for firewood. Usually the vessel was sold to another village. The bad luck was not supposed to affect the fishermen of another locality.||

There were many classes of persons whom former generations of fishermen tried to avoid when going to their boats.¶ In some places, cripples were feared. Anybody with red hair or flat feet might bring bad luck if encountered, but this could always be averted if the fisherman spoke first.§

Why certain proper names should be capable of doing harm is a mystery, but such was the firm conviction of many a Moray Firth fisherman in the past. "Ross" was a name particularly feared. When at sea anybody thus called was often referred to as "chuff 'em oot."** The Cullen fishermen

---

*Gregor. *Notes on the Folk-Lore of the North-East of Scotland.* Pp. 199, 200.

†*op. cit.* P. 200.

‡Gregor. *Folk-Lore Journal.* Vol. IV, p. 15.

||Gregor. *op. cit.* Vol. IV, p. 198.

¶It is unwise to ask for a loan of anything on a Monday from a fisherman, but he would not mind borrowing from someone else if he thought the person "lucky"!

§Gregor. *Folk-Lore Journal.* Vol. III, p. 308.

**Names ending with double consonants, e.g. Campbell or Ross, were "chiffed oot."

believed that "Anderson" and "Duffus" were dangerous words to mention at sea. The former was known as "the man who sells the coals."*

It was an almost universal superstition that women brought bad luck if met on the way to the boat before sailing.† The Rev. Walter George collected many curious beliefs and superstitions of Scottish fisher folk which were published in The Folk Lore Journal (Vol. IV). The phosphorescence often seen round a ship's mast, and usually known as St. Elmo's Light, was termed "Corvie's Aunt" or "The Covenanter" by Portessie fishermen. At Crovie, it was referred to "The Fiery Cock"; at Findochty as "Jack's Lantern," and at Nairn as "Jack o' Lantern." It was universally believed that it foretold the death of one of the relatives of the crew.

When phosphorescence appeared on the sea, Nairn fishermen used to say: "The sea's firin' ". At Buckie, when the sound of the sea was heard in the west, the fishermen would exclaim: "The chant fae th' saans o' Spey." It was looked on as a sign of good weather. The Nairn fishermen held the same opinion. They called it the "sooch o' th' sea." At Portessie the swell before a storm was known as the "win' chap."‡ In the same village the old folk used to say that the sea before any disaster from drowning had "a waichty melody," or "a dead groan." At Nairn the expression was "a waichty groan."

At Buckie and Portessie there was a common belief that the sea could not become calm until the body of a drowned person, destined for burial, had been found.

Here are some other curious superstitions, found at Portessie and elsewhere, all connected with the conviction that some object handed to one of the crew of a boat before sailing must not be opened before the boat reached home.‖

The story was told that, on one occasion a woman in Portmahomack (Ross-shire) baked a bannock, and gave it to one of the crew of a Portessie boat, with strict orders not to

---

*Hutcheson. *Days of Yore.* P. 40.

†Women on board a boat during a fishing voyage were always regarded as unlucky, and many tales are told of the disasters that befell boats which defied this superstition.

‡At Buckie "the win' chap" or buffet before "a blow" was also called "the dug afore its maister."

‖Even to-day many fisher crews do not like carrying parcels in their boats for other people, and avoid it if possible.

break it until he reached the other side of the Moray Firth, in order to get a "roon win' ". The man carefully rolled the bannock in a napkin, and put it in his breast. In climbing a rope, the bannock was broken. Until that moment the wind was quite favourable. Then it changed to a stiff breeze, and the boat only reached the shore after great difficulty.

The following story comes from Banff. It relates that a woman at Invergordon gave a fisherman a bottle, with orders that it must not be uncorked until the boat arrived home. Curiosity overcame fear. The fisherman opened the mysterious bottle. Then quite suddenly, the wind got up, and the boat was in great danger until, at last, port was reached.

At Portessie, and elsewhere on the Banffshire coast, fishermen, half a century ago, would not put in any work, such as barking nets, except when the tide was "flouwin' ". Even hens could not be set when the tide was rising.

* * * * * * *

There were lucky and unlucky boats. Some were believed to have an unlucky "spehl" in them. Shipwrights would claim to foretell the luck of a boat by the way in which a certain "spehl," or chip of wood, came off when they began work on the building. At Nairn, it was a saying that a boat built of "she-wood" sailed faster by night than by day.* To bring good luck to a new boat, the owner's wife had to put on the first "mop" of tar—at least such was a superstition at Portknockie.

Both on the East and on the West coasts, fishermen believed that a boat must always be rowed sunways when first leaving the shore. At Buckie, and in other places, it was regarded as tempting providence to turn a boat in harbour against the sun. The saying was: "Pit the boatie's heid wast aboot."

When a new boat was brought back to Crovie for the first time, those who were to do so had to set out when the tide was "flouwin' ". On the arrival of the boat, the villagers would meet her on the shore. Bread, cheese, beer or whisky were given to all. A glass of beer or spirits had to

---

*"She-oak" or chestnut is lighter than white-oak. Fishermen believed that "she-oak" had "powers."

be broken over the boat, with the following "blessing" or similar words: "I wiss this ane may gyang as lan safe oot an' in, an' catch as mony fish as the aul' ane." It was considered unlucky to go for a new boat and return without her.

At Portessie the fisher folk used to gather round a new boat. One of them would throw beer over her, sing out her name, and the onlookers cheered. Then followed the "boat feast," with beer, cheese, whisky or porter—a dinner of broth, beef, and plenty of whisky.

The superstition about flowing tides also affected other incidents of the fishing besides boats. When a new line was made, the job had to be started only on an outgoing tide, and continued without any interruption.* At Portessie the first person entering a house where a "greatline" was being made had to pay for a mutchkin of whisky, to be drunk in the house after the line was finished. But the line itself got the first glass; the whisky being poured over it.

In the larger fishing boats of the middle of the last century, the crew usually consisted of eight men, each of whom had their distinctive name. Those in the bow were known as "hanksmen." At a "boat feast" all sat together as they would be at sea. Drinking was often carried on throughout the night. A common toast was:

"Health t' men, an' death t' fish,
They're waggin' their tails, it'll pay for this."

* * * * * * *

It is difficult to say just how far the difference between the fisheries on the West and East Coast of Scotland is due to racial temperament or to economic reasons. The East Coast fishermen, who are mostly descended from Scandinavian ancestors, have inherited a belief that the sea is a "path to glory," and that "beyond the waves are strange lands and boundless wealth, waiting to be claimed by men of the necessary daring." The old Celts regarded the sea as a dark mysterious power, cruel as an evil woman, but most effective as a protection against their enemies. In short, in their attitude towards the sea, the Celt was the better poet,

---

*When barking nets before a new voyage, Friday was taboo. As far as possible barking always took place during the incoming tide.

the Norseman the better sailor.* What must not be forgotten is that most Hebridean fishermen of to-day are of mixed Norse and Celtic blood. Thus the two traits are combined.

Many of the superstitions found among fisher folk are common to both the East and the West coasts. Some are peculiar to the West Highlands, or to the Orkneys and Shetland.

For instance the Shetlanders were convinced that it was unlucky to rescue a drowning man. This is mentioned by Sir Walter Scott in *The Pirate*. "Are you mad," said the pedlar, "you that have lived sae lang in Zetland, to risk the saving of a drowning man? Wot ye not, if you bring him to life again, he will be sure to do you some capital injury?"

There was a firm belief in sea-trows among the Shetland fishermen. The trows dwelt in the ocean and came up to play. Their favourite haunt was the Vee Skerries, seven miles north-west of Papa Stour. They rose in the shape of seals. When they reached the beach they slipped off their skins, and appeared like ordinary mortals. The female trows were of great beauty. If their skins were seized, the trows were unable to escape. If shot in seal form, a tempest was sure to arise when the blood mixed with the sea. Hugh Miller, in his *Scenes and Legends of the North of Scotland*, writes that the Cromarty fishermen firmly believed in mermaids.†

In certain places it was forbidden to call things by names known on land once one was at sea. As there were many persons and objects which could not be spoken of in a boat, for instance, a minister or a rat, it was difficult for a stranger to know how to carry on a conversation without fear of danger to the boat!‡

The Rev. J. G. Campbell, in his *Superstitions of the Scottish Highlands* (1900), refers to some curious beliefs associated with fishes on the isle of Tiree. Eels were sup-

---

*Kenneth Macleod. *The Celt and the Sea*, article in *The Celtic Review*. Vol. III, p. 242.

†Many other superstitions connected with the sea are given in *Folk-Lore of Scottish Lochs and Springs* by James M. Mackinlay, 1893.

‡Salmon are called "charlies" in some places. A not uncommon name given to rabbits is "gentlemen." Rabbit Island, in the entrance to the Kyle of Tongue, Sutherlandshire, was usually referred to by Buckie fishermen as "Gentleman's Island."

Pigs were sometimes called "grumphies."

posed to grow from horse-hairs, so the natives would not eat them. Porpoises were regarded as the offspring of dog-fish. Not only on Tiree, but elsewhere in the Highlands, where fishermen agreed that the wry mouth of the flounder arose from making faces at the rock-cod. There was a tradition that this was a spell cast on the flounder by St. Columba.

This same writer records that if a fisherman beheld a mermaid at sea he threw an empty barrel overboard. He also tells us that on Tiree no fish could be given away without first sprinkling salt on it.

When the herring season seemed likely to be bad, it was a custom in some villages to dress up a cooper in flannel covered with burrs, put him on a barrow, and take him in procession round the village. At Fraserburgh, there was another mode of exorcism. Two men on horseback, both fantastically dressed, one of them playing the pipes, went round the town followed by a third man, wearing a "lum hat" hung round with herrings. Crowds followed the three men, cheering and singing.

On the Isle of Lewis, it is told how, after a good fishing season a hundred years ago, an ox or a sheep was bought by the crews of the same village. The fishermen took the beast to the spot where fish were usually landed. The oldest man led the animal to the water's edge. Kneeling on the victim, he cut the head open so that blood flowed into the sea. More blood was collected by other fishermen, who walked into the sea and sprinkled it over the waters. The carcase was cut up and divided among the poor of the district.*

In Scotland there has always been a firm conviction that it is unlucky as well as sacriligious to fish on a Sunday. Nevertheless the men in some ports were bold enough in the past to defy this taboo. There are old men who maintain that the reason why Dunbar and Stonehaven ceased to be important herring ports is because the fishermen once went to sea on Sundays. It is curious that at Prestonpans it was regarded as lucky to start fishing on the Sabbath.†

On the coast at Buchan a fisherman would burn a net by way of exorcism if he believed that his boat had been

---

*John Abercromby. *Folklore*. Vol. VI, p. 164.

†Bassett. *Legends of the Sea*. P. 442.

bewitched.* In some places, the fisher folk were convinced that if their nets got fouled, or caught in a rock, it was due to the influence of a bad fairy. To drive away the spell, one of the crew would take a piece of seaweed, or a shell, spit on it, and throw it overboard, and then spit again.†

When any forbidden name or word, such as those already mentioned, was spoken on board a fishing vessel, the crew would cry out "Cauld iron," and catch hold of the nearest bit of iron. Salmon was to be called "the big fish"; a pig "the four-fitted beastie." It was believed in some districts on the East Coast and West that certain persons could influence the weather by making knots in a particular way on a bit of rope.‡

On the return of boats to land, women were allowed to take away the fish and lines, but could not step on board the boats.

In the Outer Hebrides, when a man made his first trip at the beginning of the season, nobody was allowed to help him to land his fish. It was believed that this would drive fish away from the coast.||

* * * * * * *

There were many strange customs associated with death. In some fishing villages, onions and butter were removed from the house of a dying man. In one Aberdeenshire fishing village, not a single spadeful of earth was moved while the corpse was unburied.¶ Hens and cats were shut up until after a funeral. The bodies of those who were drowned, but not recovered, were believed to come to the surface of the water on the ninth day. Other funeral customs were similar to those found among the country folk, including the lyke-wake. This included the "kistan," that is, the laying of the body in the coffin, to which friends and near relatives of the deceased were invited, and given hospitality. Other female friends who had not been invited to the "kistan," were asked to "see the corpse." The body was watched day and

---

*Gregor. *Folklore Journal.* Vol. II, p. 308.

†*Folklore Journal.* Vol. III, p. 181.

‡*Revue des traditions populaires.* Vol. IV, p. 663.

||Article by A. Goodrich Freer, *Folk-lore Journal* Vol. X.

¶Gregor. *Notes on the Folk-lore of the North-East of Scotland.* Pp. 206-207.

night, to keep away evil spirits. The time was mostly spent in reading the Bible. Conversation was carried on in low voices. New pipes and tobacco were provided for the men, also whisky. About midnight a plentiful meal of tea, beer and bread and cheese was served. In some fishing villages bread and water were placed in the room in which the body had lain the night after the funeral.*

On the West Coast, there are many other traditions associated with death at sea. The sea is generous, but there are limits to its generosity. "The sea," says an old Gaelic rhyme, "will search the four russet divisions of the universe to find the graves of her children." For this reason it is believed that a body washed ashore must be buried as near the shore as possible, so that the sea may "recover her own," if such be her will.† There is a legend that the neglect of this precaution once caused a great flood in the Hebrides. Little more than a hundred years ago, so it is related, an unknown body was washed ashore on North Uist. It was laid to rest in the graveyard, but at twilight "a mysterious looking barge glided into the bay." Three of the crew marched silently up to the cemetery, opened the grave, carried off the body, and then disappeared into the darkness of the ocean.‡

This story is typical of the Celtic attitude towards the sea—a consciousness of its mystery, and utterly different to the crude pagan superstitions of the East Coast fisher folk. The Celt is often so preoccupied with dreaming about the sea, that he has no urge to make money out of it! There is more of the poet in the typical Hebridean fisherman than the business-man. It is doubtful if the sea ever inspired the Buchan or Shetland fishermen to poetry such as the Dunvegan sea-hymn.¶

Thou who dwellest,
In the heights above,
O succour us in the depths below;
Vouchsafe to us a day-breeze
As Thou Thyself wouldst wish,
Vouchsafe to us a night-breeze
As we ourselves would choose.

---

*Gregor. *op. cit.* Pp. 210-216.

†"*The Celt and the Sea*"—article by Kenneth Macleod, in *The Celtic Review*. Vol. III, p. 247.

‡*op. cit.* P. 247.

‖"*Rescued on the Island of Eigg*," by Kenneth Macleod, and printed in the article already mentioned. P. 251.

May the clouds hide us,
May the moon shine on the foe,
Be we to windward
And becalmed as they;
O keep firmly tethered
All sudden blasts and accidents—
And leave the rest to us.

Or again, it would seem quite out of place for any East Coast fisherman to invoke Our Lady in the words of the Clan-Ranald "sea prayer," usually known as "The Dawn Prayer."*

"Fragrant maiden of the sea,
Thou art full of graces,
And the Great White King is with thee.
Blessed art thou, blessed art thou,
Blessed art thou among women.
Thy breath steering my prayer,
It will reach the haven white;
Let me beseech thy gentle Son
To whom thou gavest knee and suck
To be with us,
To be on watch,
To be awake;"

These two quotations typify the difference between the Norse and Celtic attitude towards the sea. The East Coast fishermen, at least those of past generations, had a fear of the sea, and their whole life was bound up with taboos and superstitions, nevertheless it has a source of wealth waiting to be claimed by any man who had the daring. But the West Coast fisherman was far more conscious of the mystery of the ocean—she was a spirit that had to be wooed. Pagan superstitions were mellowed and absorbed into Catholicism, as in this prayer: chanted by some fishermaiden "to whom even the seagulls could bring no tidings, good or bad, of her dear one":—

"O Virgin, pity me to-night
If his shroud be the tangle,
If his couch a sandy hollow,
If the seals his wake-attendants,
If the fish his waxen candles,
If his harp the croon of waves."†

---

*Taken down by Kenneth Macleod on the Island of Eigg.
†*op. cit.* P. 245.

Having given so much space to recording superstitions whose sources were pagan, Catholic or satanic, it is important to stress the fact that a firm belief in them was not incompatible with a firm allegiance to the doctrines and practices of orthodox Presbyterianism. For instance, just over a hundred years ago the parish minister of Latheron, Caithness, wrote that "it is not unusual where the boats having individuals of acknowledged piety, for the crew to engage in worship after shooting their nets. On these occasions a portion of a psalm is sung, followed by prayer, and the effect is represented as truly solemn and heart stirring, as the melodious strains of Gaelic music, carried along the surface of the waters, several boats being sometimes engaged, spread through the whole fleet."*

J. M'Gibbon relates in *The Fisherfolk of Buchan* (p. 76) that it was quite common, during the "Revival" of 1860, to hear the crews of the East Coast fishing boats bursting into a hymn or psalm when leaving the harbour. When putting out to sea they usually sang the twenty-third psalm. If the boat had a good catch they generally sang the hymn "*O God of Bethel, by Whose Hand.*" Far away over the sea could be heard the voices of the fishermen, singing, *Jesu Lover of my Soul,* or *Rock of Ages, cleft for me,* as they shot their herring nets. Many skippers would lead their crews in prayer before shooting the nets.

Previous to the middle of the last century, the fisher folk, taken as a whole, seem to have been little influenced by any form of organised Christianity, except in a few parishes. This is the impression formed after studying the many volumes of the *Old Statistical Account.* The ministers who were responsible for compiling the accounts of their respective parishes refer far more often to their vices than to their virtues. The reader gathers that the fishermen and their families were a rough and immoral crowd, and almost everywhere given over to drink and smuggling.

A change swept over the fishing communities about 1859, due to the "Revival Movement" which took root in Scotland, having reached this country from America by way of Northern Ireland. The chief leader of this religious movement in the North-East of Scotland was a Peterhead cooper, James Turner. It was claimed that he "converted"

***New Statistical Account of Scotland.* Vol. XV, p. 88.

more than eight thousand persons along the coasts. Both towns and villages were affected. In more than one fishing village, it is recorded that James Turner kept on preaching and praying half the night until everybody had "gone forrit," that is gone up to the "penitents' form" to confess their sins in public and "accepted salvation." The kirks and other places of worship were now too small for their congregations. In many places the newly converted, finding orthodox religion cold and unemotional, formed themselves into groups of "The Brethren," and seceded from other Protestant sects.

Hardly had the first Revival Movement had time to cool down than the Salvation Army appeared on the coast. The disciples of General Booth launched their spiritual offensive among the Scottish fisher folk with all the panoply of banners, brass bands and the waving of tambourines. It must have been a shock to find spiritual religion bound up with scarlet jerseys, picturesque poke-bonnets and peaked caps. Lurid posters displayed reference to "Blood and Fire." At first the East Coast fisher folk were cautious. Such unfamiliar ceremonial alarmed them. But their highly emotional temperament, once the repressions and inhibitions had been lifted, found that this new manifestation of religion was more satisfying than the narrow sectarianism of the Open or Close Brethren, or the respectable atmosphere of the parish kirk. Some of the hardest "cases" who had failed to be kindled by the fires of previous Revival Movements were melted by the faith and persistent preaching of the Salvation Army.

About 1921, after the first world-war, another "spiritual offensive" began among the fisher commuunities—this time during the East Anglian herring season. The leader was Jock Troup, who had heard the Voice of God bidding him go forth and preach Salvation. Once the drifters returned to Scotland, the movement spread through the towns and villages on the North-East coast. Men, women and children were caught up in this whirlwind of revivalism. One of the natives of a Moray Firth village is said to have told a reporter who wanted "copy" for his paper: "The folk up the brae have heard nae call to repentance an' consecration for the Lord's service an' they doot if we have. Aye, they're har' and creetical up th' toon. They're expectin' that if the Lord wants them He'll come an' ring them up specially on their telephones. They dinna understan' that doon th' brae th' aerials are aye oot, an' that he carries a receiver in his heart to catch th' first whisper o' th' Spirit."

Sudden conversions took place. Hungry, eager faces would gaze up at the passionate words of a fiery young evangelist. His preaching was often interrupted by ejaculations of "Amen" and "Hallelujah!" There was much hymn singing, endless prayers and petitions for those whose hearts were still hardened. Converts stood up and "gave testimony." Men and women joined hands as they sang stirring choruses, such as *"Will your anchor hold?"* or *"Throw out the life-line."* An irresistible influence drove weather-beaten skippers, young deck-hands and countless lassies up the hall to the penitents' form.

In later years there have been similar Revival Movements among the fisher folk, but on a less intensive scale. It must be admitted that the present generation is less religiously inclined. For many—but not all—the cinema wields a more potent influence than either the kirk or the chapel. Film stars have a stronger appeal than evangelists.

* * * * * *

At the present time the majority of Scots fisherfolk are at least nominal members of the Church of Scotland, although it would be hard to say just how many are communicants. In parts of the Highlands and the Outer Hebrides they will be found among the congregations of the Free Kirk and other smaller groups of Presbyterians. The Scottish Episcopal Church has a very small membership among fisher families, except in the Buchan District of Aberdeenshire, where this body has always been strong. On the islands of South Uist, Barra, Eriskay, Eigg and Canna, also in the mainland districts of Knoydart and Moydart, the majority of the fishermen-crofters are devout Catholics.

Fishermen and their families are also supporters of the Salvation Army. In some places they worship with the Baptists, Congregationalists and Methodists. They tend to be drawn to other smaller Christian sects, such as the Assemblies of God, the Churches of Christ, or Jehovah's Witnesses.

In parts of Orkney and Shetland, the Western Isles, the Black Isle, all along the south side of the Moray Firth, and at Eyemouth, there are halls belonging to one or other group of "The Brethren," largely made up of fisher families. Their places of worship are often designated "Assemblies" or "Churches of God." This sect, with no central organisation, originated about 1827 from a desire for more simplicity and fervour in religion. One of the chief centres of the movement was Plymouth, hence the name "Plymouth Brethren" by which the adherents are usually known.

In the middle of the last century there was a division between the "Open Brethren," who associate with other Christians, and the "Exclusive Brethren," who practise complete separation from all those not of their fellowship. Both divisions inevitably break up into further groups, since all male members have the right to preach and there is no organised ministry. The movement eventually spread from East Anglia and took a firm hold among the fisher folk in those parts of Scotland already mentioned. The movement is anti-clerical; separation from the world and its pleasures is insisted upon; the Bible is regarded as infallible, and belief in the speedy return of Christ is emphasised*

The People's Mission at Fraserburgh, formerly in Peterhead, is another of the evangelical sects which has drawn away members from the Church of Scotland. The British Women's Templars Association is also strong on the Buchan coast. Then there is the Faith Mission, whose "pilgrims" preach in the fishing towns and villages, holding missions and evangelistic campaigns, without any permanent quarters.

* * * * * * *

The spiritual and social welfare of Scots fisherfolk is attended to by several organisations, the chief of which is the *Royal National Mission to Deep Sea Fishermen*, founded in 1881. At the present time it maintains Institutes at Aberdeen, Peterhead, Wick and Lerwick. Each establishment is in charge of a Mission Skipper, and provides board, lodging and recreation, as well as spiritual ministrations of an interdenominational character. Until the second world-war the Mission kept in service one or

---

**A Christian Year Book* (1947 edition), p. 71.

more hospital ships. Recently a converted landing craft—*Sir Edward P. Wills*—was put into commission. This large vessel is fitted with recreation rooms and a canteen. She voyages round from one fishing centre to another according to the season. The splendid work done by the R.N.M.D.S.F., which also includes first-aid and dressing stations, has been of immense value to thousands of Scots fishermen and fish-workers—male and female—for nearly seventy years.

The *Missions to Seamen,* a Church of England organisation, did not start work in Scottish ports until 1914. Its chaplains and lay-readers have done much good work on behalf of fisherfolk at Campbeltown, Stromness and Lerwick. The *Mission to Fisherfolk*—another Episcopalian Society has been ministering to the bodies and souls of fishermen and fishworkers for about seventy years. Rest Huts and Dressing Stations were opened at Lerwick, Stronsay, Kirkwall, Peterhead, Buckie, also at Yarmouth and Lowestoft during the autumn herring season. Some of them are now closed, being required no longer. Similar in scope is the Church of Scotland Mission to Workers in the Herring Industry, commonly known as "*The Work among the Fisherfolk.*" At one time it counted a staff of about thirty ladies and eight ministers, working at the chief centres of the herring fisheries, and bringing spiritual, social and medical aid to men and women. The Church of Scotland has recently opened St Andrew's Institute at Yarmouth, to replace the original building bombed during the last war.

The *British Sailor's Society,* established in 1818, has always concentrated its work among the Mercantile Marine, but during the second world war it ran a Hostel in Buckie, which was a great boon to the Norwegian fishermen who were then so numerous in this port. The B.S.S. still has a Sailor's Home in Aberdeen, but this is mainly patronised by merchant seamen. The Society will soon open a Home at Stornoway, where not much has been done hitherto for the spiritual and social welfare of fishermen. There is a *Scandinavian Seamen's Institute* in Aberdeen, with a Port Chaplain, which carries on a good work among the Faroese fishermen who are now such frequent visitors to this port.

About forty years ago St Margaret's Catholic Rest Hut and Dressing Station for fish-workers was opened at Lerwick. After being closed during the last war the Hut is now being run as a social centre during the summer fishing season by the *Catholic Women's League* of Aberdeen. The priest from Kirkwall resides at Lerwick while the herring fishing is at its height to attend to his migratory flock, less numerous now than in the past.

CHAPTER IV.

THE EAST COAST.

There are three fishing ports in Berwickshire—*Burnmouth, Eyemouth* and *St. Abbs.* Burnmouth is a hamlet nestling beneath the cliffs, where lobsters and crabs are landed in large quantities. Eyemouth's connection with the fishing industry dates from the thirteenth century. The monks of Coldingham obtained the rights of fishing off this coast. The white fisheries began to develop about 1750. Herring curing was started after the Napoleonic wars. By 1850 Eyemouth became one of the chief herring ports in Scotland. A considerable amount of white fishing is still carried on, but herring is no longer important. *Dunbar* ranked as the main herring port in this country throughout the eighteenth century. Today it is better known as a popular holiday resort. *North Berwick* has shared the same fate. *Port Seton* has superseded *Cockenzie,* its near neighbour. Here we find a fleet of seine-net boats. *Fisherrow*—now part of Musselburgh—was a busy little port about a hundred years ago, and shows sign of reviving. *Leith* is the port of registry for fifty-nine steam trawlers. *Newhaven* has been a fishing centre since the fifteenth century. Its original name was "Our Lady's Port of Grace." There is a tradition that the first fisher families came from Flanders.

Very few of the old houses remain here. A fleet of up-to-date motor vessels with seine-nets land their catches in the small harbour. *Granton* has a spacious harbour, mostly used by steam trawlers.

On the north side of the Firth of Forth are several ports, where fishing has long since declined. They include *Burntisland, Kinghorn, Kirkcaldy, Dysart* and *West Wemyss.* Further east lies *Buckhaven,* at one time one of the chief centres of the herring trade in Scotland. Here, as elsewhere—coal mining and other industries have killed fishing. The same decline has not taken place in some of the Fife ports further east. *Largo* is derelict, but *St. Monans, Pittenweem* and *Anstruther* (incorporating the much more ancient village of *Cellardyke*) are still busy enough with herring and white fishing according to

DRIFTERS AT BUCKIE.

the season. These burghs have been bound up with sea fishing since the Middle Ages. St. Monans has a famous yard where fishing vessels are built. Whaling was carried on at Anstruther during the early years of the last century. *Crail* now concentrates on shell fish. Two hundred years ago it maintained its own "Admiral Deputy" who had the right to try all offences committed by persons employed in the then prosperous herring fisheri s. *St. Andrews*—as a port—is derelict, but its history as a fishing centre goes back over a thousand years.

Dundee has never been one of the leading fishing ports, except for whaling during the first half of the nineteenth century. At the present time, a fleet of seven steam-trawlers is based here. *Broughty Ferry, East* and *West Haven* have long since ceased to count. *Arbroath* fishermen were encouraged by the Benedictine monks of the great abbey before the Reformation. The suppression of the monastery seems to have ruined the local fisheries. Eventually they revived. At the time of writing, Arbroath manages to provide Dundee and other towns in Angus with most of the fish sold in their shops. A few miles eastward is *Auchmithie*, a tiny derelict hamlet, described by Sir Walter Scott in *The Antiquary*. *Ferryden*, opposite Montrose, once supplied the London market with dried haddock. Throughout the seventeenth century the fishing industry brought wealth to *Montrose*. Most of the catch was exported to Germany, Holland, France and England. Only a few seine-net boats now fish from here. Salmon netting is probably more remunerative.

On the Mearns coast lie *Johnshaven, Gourdon, Bervie* and *Catterline*. With the exception of Gourdon, all these villages are now moribund so far as fishing is concerned. *Stonehaven* has an ancient history as a fishing port, but fluctuating at all periods. Between Stonehaven and Aberdeen, situated on rocky cliffs, are the villages of *Skateraw, Muchalls, Downies, Portlethen, Findon* and *Cove*. Each once had its own fleet of small boats that were hauled up the cliffs when not at sea. To-day few fishermen or boats are to be found anywhere on this stretch of coast.

Salmon has been caught at *Aberdeen* since the thirteenth century. Pickled salmon were exported in large quantities during the Middle Ages, not only to England but to many countries on the continent of Europe. It was so cheap in the seventeenth that farm-servants used to complain that they were given too much salmon. Very little attention was paid to other kinds of fishing before the close of the eighteenth century. White fish was brought into Aberdeen from many of the adjacent villages. Trawling was started in 1882. The line fishermen of *Torry* and *Footdee* rebelled. They tried hard to force the authorities to stop what they described as "an outrageous method of catching fish." But to no purpose—trawling had come to stay. In 1889 there were thirteen trawlers working from Aberdeen. By 1929 their number had risen to over two hundred, their crews amounting to nearly 28,000 men. At the present time 193 trawlers and 22 great-liners are based here. Foreign trawlers —mostly Faroese—land their catches at Aberdeen. Seine-net motor boats, mostly registered at other ports, find this a better base to work from at certain seasons. The fishing industry has led to the establishment of ice-producing factories, fish-meal and fertilising plants, fish-canning and paste-making factories. Fishing vessels, including many for foreign countries, are built and repaired.

Between Aberdeen and Peterhead lie the villages of *Newburgh, Collieston, Whinnyfold, Port Erroll* and *Boddam,* all of which have now ceased to have any commercial importance. Boddam, more than all of them, conveys a sense of dereliction.

Peterhead only developed into a fishing centre in the eighteenth century. Previous to that, the adjacent village of *Buchanhaven*—now absorbed into the burgh—was more important. Herring fishing was started in 1818. It was secondary to whaling which at the height of its prosperity employed between two and three hundred men and boys. By 1850, Peterhead had become the second herring port in Scotland. The number of resident fishermen increased from 407 in 1855 to 990 in 1928. At the present time about 190 vessels, including 88 steam-drifters, are registered here. Peterhead in 1948 could claim to have the largest steam-drifter fleet in Scotland. There has been a great development in seine-net fishing by up-to-date motor vessels in recent years. Crosse and Blackwell Ltd. have important fish-canning and paste-making factories in the town.

There are no fishing centres between Peterhead and Fraserburgh other than the villages of *St. Combs, Inver-*

allochy and *Cairnbulg*. None of them have harbours. Most of their resident fishermen go to sea in vessels working from *Fraserburgh*.

This busy town is now the chief herring port on the mainland of Scotland. Before the latter end of the eighteenth century, the fisher folk had their homes in the adjacent village of Broadsea. Herring curing started at Fraserburgh in 1810. Five eyars later curing yards had been opened, and the first consignments of herring shipped abroad. A harbour was built and enlarged again and again to find room for the ever increasing fleet. The most prosperous years of the herring industry were between 1870 and 1900. Fraserburgh harbour during the summer months—even to-day—is a sight worth seeing. On an average more than two hundred drifters land herring every day. White fish is also landed in considerable quantities; caught both by seine-nets and lines.

Fraserburgh has killed the ports of *Sandhaven, Pittulie* and above all, *Rosehearty,* which lies westward. A century ago Rosehearty showed signs of rivalling Fraserburgh as the chief herring port on the north-east coast. To-day its two harbours are practically empty. There are a few lobster fishermen at Sandhaven. *Pennan,* hidden away beneath red sandstone cliffs, is a picturesque but now derelict fishing village. On the east side of Gamrie Bay lies *Crovie,* with an equally romantic setting. *Gardenstown,* nestling below precipitous cliffs on the other side of the Bay, is a go-ahead village. The fishermen keep their larger seine-net boats and drifters in Macduff harbour. Shell fish are another source of profit.

Macduff started life as a hamlet about 1733, when the Earl of Fife encouraged Banff fishermen to settle on the east side of the Deveron. Here he erected a small harbour and built houses. A town arose, the harbour was enlarged, and the new town prospered. By 1928 there were over four hundred fishermen belonging to Macduff. To-day seine-net fishing, carried on with about forty up-to-date motor-vessels, is the chief occupation. There are boat-building and engineering works.

Banff harbour, once the centre of an important herring fishing and coastal trade, is now more or less derelict, except for a boat-building yard. *Whitehills* is a flourishing village, just as much alive to-day as in the eighteenth century, with a good harbour and a fleet of seine-net craft. The harbour at *Portsoy* and the surrounding warehouses are a silent witness of the maritime activities of this port in past ages. Only a few small boats are found here at the present time. *Sandend* is more like a toy village, with its tiny harbour, but is very much alive. *Cullen* was a busy seaport five hundred years ago. Herring curing was started in 1815. The peak of prosperity was reached about 1880. As a port, Cullen is practically dead, but it still has a fairly large resident population of fishermen. *Portknockie* and *Findochty*, further west, have grown up on the herring industry. So also has *Portessie*, which lacks a harbour, but which is inhabited almost entirely by fisher folk.

Buckie, until fairly recently, had the largest fleet of steam-drifters in Scotland, but priority is now held by Peterhead. However it is probable that the burgh can still claim to have the largest number of resident fishermen. The first houses were built during the seventeenth century. Herring curing was started soon after the Napoleonic wars. The first harbour—no longer used—was at *Buckpool*. By 1880 there were about 150 boats here. Unlike some other ports, Buckie held on to its steam drifters during the lean years after the first World War, confident that the export herring trade would regain its former prosperity. Eventually many of the vessels had to be sold at a loss or broken up. There was great distress and much poverty. The harbour is spacious. Shipbuilding and repairing is carried on. To-day hardly any herring is landed at Buckie. Seine-netting is now carried on by a number of fine new vessels. During the second world war Buckie became the home of many Norwegian fishermen and their families. There were times when one could find more Norwegian boats in the harbour than Scottish. *Portgordon*, with a harbour dating from 1797, is now rather the home of many fishermen, who keep their vessels at Buckie.

Lossiemouth, the chief fishing centre of Morayshire, started to develop in 1819 when the first herring curing yards were opened. It was the first port in Scotland to adopt the now almost universal Danish seine-net in 1921. So profitable was this new method of fishing that before long, Lossiemouth had sold practically all its drifters and concentrated on seine-net fishing. It retains the reputation

WICK.

for being one of the most go-ahead ports in Scotland. *Hopeman* and *Burghead* are smaller places which still carry on in a quiet way. *Findhorn*, once an important centre of the herring industry, no longer figures in the Reports of the Fishery Board. *Nairn* has developed from an ancient fishing village into a fashionable golfing and holiday resort. Herring curing was started in 1828, but ceased about 1850. A new harbour was built after the first World War, but not much fishing is carried on here to-day. *Inverness* was famous for the fish landed during the eighteenth century when shoals of herring came into the Beauly Firth. It hardly counts as a fishing centre at the present time.

On the north side of the Moray Firth, there are very few places where fishing is of any commercial importance in these days. *Avoch*, on the Black Isle, is a village with a long history, and still prosperous in a small way. There is a tradition that the original inhabitants came from Wales or Cornwall. Throughout the eighteenth century Avoch fishermen were famous for their hardiness, skill and industry. Few ports have declined so much as *Cromarty*. To-day it is difficult to picture it as one of the chief centres of the herring trade in Scotland, which was the case in the seventeenth century. By 1839 the herring shoals had vanished from the coasts. The fisher folk were reduced to dire poverty. Most of them migrated elsewhere. *Hilton, Shandwick, Balintore* and *Portmahomack*—all of them north of Cromarty—are villages with more of a past than a present. *Helmsdale* developed into a busy centre of the herring fisheries early in the last century They are now almost forgotten, but the port maintains a fleet of motor vessels that do fairly well by seine-netting.

The south coast of Caithness is full of deserted harbours, where a hundred years ago fleets of small boats put out to sea at all seasons of the year. To-day *Achastle*, *Forse, Latheronwheel* and *Dunbeath* are more or less abandoned. *Lybster* has a fine harbour, but very few boats are left.

Wick did not start herring fishing until about the middle of the eighteenth century. Within a few years, boats were coming here from southern ports every summer. The first harbour was built in 1810. By 1862 more than one thousand boats were taking part in the annual herring fisheries. So great was the congestion that the harbour had to be enlarged again. Until the first World War, Wick remained one of the chief herring ports in Britain. With the loss of foreign markets for cured herring it declined rapidly. In 1948, the port took on a new lease of life, although most of the drifters working from here came from other districts, many of them from England.

North of Wick are to be found the now practically derelict villages of *Staxigoe, Auckingill, Keiss* and *Freswick.* At one time all of them maintained a fleet of small boats. Staxigoe was formerly much more important than Wick in the early days of the herring fisheries on this coast.

CHAPTER V.

THE ORKNEYS AND SHETLAND.

The Orkneys abound in fish, but the inhabitants of these islands have never developed fishing on a serious commercial basis. In the past, the Orcadian was a farmer who fished occasionally instead of a fisherman who farmed, which is still the best way to describe the average Shetlander.

The *Old Statistical Account of Scotland* relates that, at the close of the eighteenth century, the inhabitants used to catch fish for home consumption when they could spare time from farming or kelp burning. Farming suffered because many able-bodied young men left the islands to serve in the whaling ships or in the Mercantile Marine. We learn that at *Kirkwall* the poorer classes laid in a supply of dried fish every summer, which was eaten during the winter months. Fifty years later, lobsters had become a great source of profit. Over forty boats were regularly employed in this fishing. Most of the catch was taken to London in smacks.

Stromness has always been a nursery for seafarers. In 1700 it had two boats that sailed as far as Barra for cod and ling. Every year a vessel called at Stromness to take the dried fish to Leith or Norway. In 1790, London was regularly supplied with lobsters from this port. Many men were employed in the whalers that went to Greenland, Hudson's Bay and the Davis Straits. In 1845 about three hundred seamen from Stromness served in the whaling ships. Herring fishing and curing had been started before that date. On most of the southern islands the farmers engaged in fishing at certain seasons, while other men earned their living in the whaling ships. On *South Ronaldshay* more than two hundred boats took part in the herring fishing. The parish minister complained that the curers had increased drunkenness by giving each crew a bottle of whisky daily. White fish was taken in the spring and autumn. It was dried in the open air and stored for winter use.

Elsewhere the inhabitants of the islands were mostly farmer-fishermen. At *Stronsay* herring curing was started in 1814. By 1845 the islands were invaded by hundreds of fishworkers every summer. Stronsay continued to be the only large herring curing centre until shortly before the second World-War. In 1948 no herring was landed in the Orkneys. To-day the only important commercial fishing is lobsters. In 1948 over 374,000 lobsters were landed in this District as against 119,329 in 1938.

* * * * * * *

For more than a thousand years, the Shetlanders have usually managed to live in comparative comfort by fishing in summer and working on the land in winter. Herring fishing has been carried on off Shetland from time immemorial. Some of the lairds were exporting herring to Hamburg early in the eighteenth century. The deep-sea white fishing (the "*haaf*" fishing) was controlled by German merchants from Hamburg, Bremen and Lübeck. A few English and Scottish merchants also took a share in the *haaf* fisheries, but it was mostly in the hands of the "Dutchmen," as the North-German merchants were called locally. Foreign vessels fished off the islands and carried off "prodigious quantities" of cod and ling. In 1784 it was recorded that over four hundred foreign ships, each of about a hundred tons, were employed in this fishing. They salted and barrelled their catches at sea. The *haaf* fishing was usually carried on by local open boats from stations situated on the outer islands or on any spot near the fishing grounds. This was important for the Shetland fishermen who sold their catches to the merchants, relied more on oar than on sail.

Sometimes these open boats went so far off that even Rönis Hill, the highest point in Shetland, disappeared below the horizon before they set their lines. There are recorded instances when the "sixerns" from the Skerries or Fetlar were hauling within sight of Norway. The smaller "fourareens" generally returned home every night. Ling, tusk and cod were the most valuable fish taken. They were dried in the sun and packed in dry-stone cellars until shipped abroad. It was not until about 1876 that the Shetland fishermen began to buy second-hand decked boats from the Moray Firth ports. These more sea-worthy vessels gradually replaced the native craft. The older men never worried about taking a compass on board. If a fog came on, they put their faith in the "*Moder-di*," a sort of under-current that always runs towards the land.

Cod fishing with half-decked smacks was carried on as far back as the eighteenth century. These vessels did not venture very far away until after the discovery of the Regent's Bank, off Foula, in 1817. Some years later they started to sail to the even more distant Rockall grounds. About 1832 the Faröes were visited for the first time. The nearer fishing grounds were abandoned. From 1846 to about 1850 some Shetland smacks and schooners ventured as far north as the Davis Straits. But the cod found in these regions was not so good in quality as that taken off the Faröes. This mode of fishing came to an end about 1897. There was no other district in Scotland where a fleet of smacks was fitted out for the deep-sea cod fisheries.

Lobster and oyster fishing was carried on at one time, but never to the same extent. Whaling was engaged in at different periods. There were four whaling stations in Shetland. Most of the men employed were Norwegians.

It was not until the early years of the nineteenth century that the Shetlanders themselves began to take any active part in the herring fisheries. For over two hundred years they had been content to catch no more than a few barrels of herring for their landlords—"the gleanings of the Hollanders' busses," as John Smith described them in his *Trade and Fishing of Great Britain* (1661). About 1820 boats from the Moray Firth and the Orkneys started to fish for herring off Shetland. Six years later, curing began at *Lerwick.* This port has always been the chief centre of the herring industry. As far back as 1701, John Brand wrote in his *Brief Description of Orkneys, Zetland, etc.*, that "so thick do the ships lie in the Sound, that they say that men might go from one side of the Sound, stepping from ship to ship." About 1880 it was a common sight in the summer to find off Lerwick between three and four hundred Dutch "loggers," "sloops" and "bomschuits," besides all types of vessels from Scottish and English ports, not to mention a few French, Belgian, Swedish, Danish, Norwegian and Icelandic drifters. To complete the cosmopolitan atmosphere of the narrow streets of Lerwick on a Saturday night there were the Gaelic speaking women and girls from the West Highlands and boys from Donegal.

The curing yards in course of time spread round the north end of the harbour, far past *Grimister* and across the Sound on the Isle of *Bressay,* each station with its wooden jetty. Adjacent to them were rows of wooden huts in which the female fish-workers lodged. In prosperous years before the first World-War, and in some seasons after 1918, in addition to the crews of the drifters, which often numbered well over six thousand men, the herring industry gave employment in Lerwick to about four thousand shore workers —gutters, coopers, carters, labourers and sailors. Herring curing was carried on in a smaller scale at *Scalloway, Whalsay, Levenwick, Skerries, Cullivoe* and *Mid Yell,* etc.

Between 1939 and 1945 enemy air-activity made it too dangerous to carry on herring fishing. A few small local craft worked in the bays and voes and landed a very limited amount for home consumption. Since 1946 the Herring Industry Board has been trying to revive the industry at Lerwick by various schemes, including new methods of processing herring. In 1948 there were 59 motor boats and 61 steam drifters fishing from this port. Among the machinery set up by the Board are a quick-freezing plant and cold store for fresh herring; a sharp-freezing plant for kippers, and experimental kippering kilns. A not very successful trial of winter herring fishing was made in 1948. There was a factory for making herring oil and meal as long as sixty years ago. More of these could be opened. The object of these and other experiments is to co-ordinate the different sections of the industry at Lerwick, so that all concerned should work at full capacity for the whole of the season, and obtain adequate returns for their efforts.

There has been a great development of seine-net fishing in Shetland since the second world war, which seems likely to become as important as line-fishing in the past century.

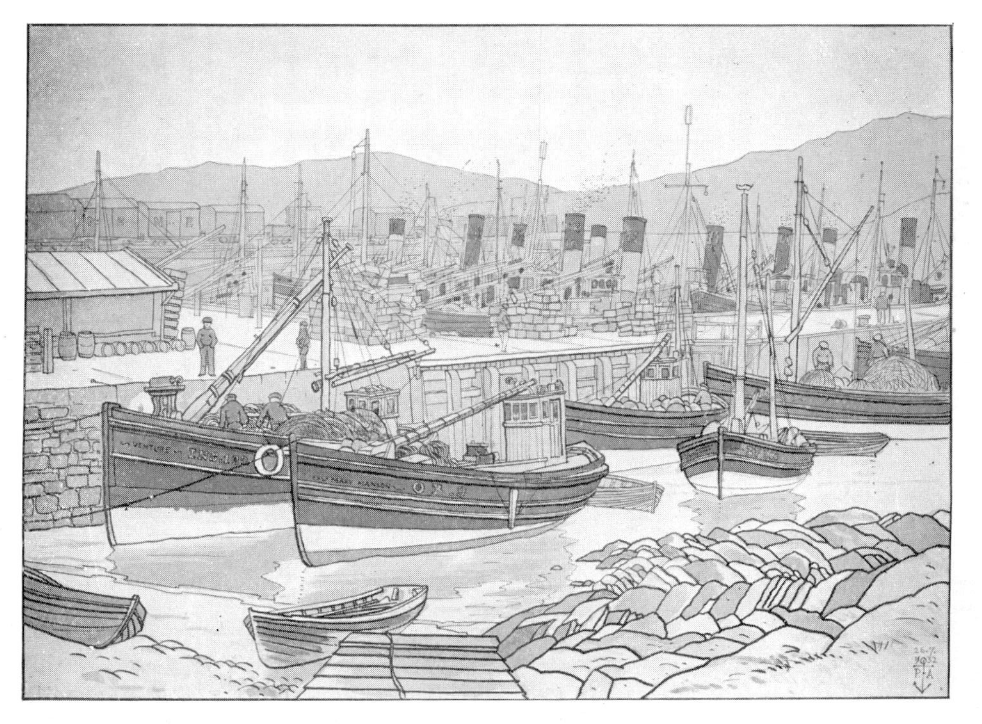

MALLAIG.

CHAPTER VI.

THE NORTH AND WEST COASTS—MAINLAND AND ISLANDS.

White fish formed the chief export from *Thurso* at the close of the eighteenth century. Cured herring was shipped direct to London, and even to the West Indies from about the same period. English lobster smacks worked in the Pentland Firth. The local fishermen often protested that they were being robbed by these foreigners. Actually there were very few whole-time fishermen on the north coast of Caithness and Sutherland. There are even less to-day, although lobsters are still fairly profitable in some places.

When reading the *New Statistical Account of Scotland* one forms the impression that almost every farm and croft owned a few boats a hundred years ago. Both white fish and herring were caught by these fishermen-crofters. They dried or cured the fish to add to their meagre diet in winter. Their way of living had not changed much from what is described in the *Old Statistical Account* which appeared about half a century earlier. During the last decade of the eighteenth century there were very few professional fishermen between *Tongue* and *Lochinver*. But as one parish minister stated, "if tugging an oar in a boisterous sea can be called the accomplishment of seamen, in this event all the tenants of the present noble proprietors along the coast are seamen." Much the same could be said to-day.

Very little information is given in either the *Old* or *New Statistical Accounts* concerning the fisheries on the west coast of the counties of Ross and Invernes. *Ullapool* was established as a herring centre by the British Fisheries Association in 1788. This organisation founded other stations in Loch Broom, at *Isle Martin* and on *Tanera Island*. *Glenelg,* on the Sound of Sleat, was also much frequented during the latter half of the eighteenth century. By 1945 the once fairly prosperous herring fisheries on the Isle of Skye had declined. The people were reduced to poverty and destitution. The same story is told of many other districts. Within recent years the herring fisheries on the North West coast have revived. *Ullapool, Gairloch* and *Lochinver* have become important as mainland landing ports, largely due to the development of road transport. Seine-net boats from the East Coast are also using Ullapool as their base. *Kyle of Lochalsh* lost its former importance as a herring port, partly owing to naval operations during the second world-war.

There are few professional fishermen between Loch Nevis, Inverness-shire, and the Firth of Lorn. This coast-line is included in the Fishery District of Fort William, like-wise the Island of *Eigg, Rum, Canna, Tiree, Coll, Lismore* and *Mull.* Most of the crofters on the coasts own boats and sometimes fish with hand-lines at certain seasons. *Mallaig* has a good harbour, built by the West Highland Railway Company after the Fort William line was extended into North Morar in 1901. No other port on the north-west coast is so well adapted for landing fish. Mallaig developed into a busy centre of the herring industry before and after the first world-war. Until 1939 it was largely frequented by East Coast drifters. Both herring and white-fish are still landed here.

Tobermory and *Salen* in Mull have always been famous for the amount of lobsters exported. Between the two world wars *Oban* was an important base for drifters. To-day it is more used by trawlers and seine-net vessels working off the West Coast.

Throughout the eighteenth and the first half of the nineteenth centuries, it was always the same story of the Highlands and Islands being unable to make use of the vast quantities of fish waiting to be caught, especially her-ring. In 1765 the inhabitants of *Fort William* were des-cribed as "a lazy, indolent set of people," who did not take advantage of the cod, ling and herring shoals that were abundant in Loch Linnhe. There was more than enough fish in the sea, but few fishermen with boats. It is much the same story to-day. But it cannot be said that the men are "lazy and indolent!" Many would like to venture out to sea if they had larger boats. The best they can do with the craft at their disposal is to catch lobsters.

* * * * * * *

It has largely been foreigners who have made money out of fish caught off the Outer Hebrides. In a previous chapter it has been related how the French, Dutch and English tried hard to gain control of the Hebridean fisheries during the seventeenth and eighteenth centuries. A hundred and fifty years ago the fishermen of these islands were in a bad way. They lacked adequate boats. The Salt Laws prevented profitable fishing. Smuggling was regarded as being more lucrative. The situation had improved slightly by 1845. White fishing for cod and ling had become the chief occupation for most of the male inhabitants of the parish of Stornoway and other parts of Lewis. Nearly every farm and croft by the shore owned one or more boats. Most of them were too small to go far off in search of herring. The majority of the people on North Uist were miserably poor. When other food was lacking, they gathered cockles and made them into a stew with milk and oatmeal. The Barra fishermen seem to have been more enterprising. They ventured further out to sea in their open boats for cod and ling. The fish, caught with great-lines, was dried and then taken to Glasgow by these same boats. Much of this dried fish was exported to Spain. The hardy fisherman, mostly of Norse origin, on the Butt of Lewis, rivalled the Barra men for skill and daring. But in 1870 the position of most Hebridean fishermen was far from secure. Many were in debt to the curers who supplied them with boats and gear. The majority of the men lacked capital to buy larger boats. They could only earn a living by catching lobsters.

It was not until about 1850 that the Hebrideans began to take up herring fishing themselves and tried to compete with the boats from the Moray Firth that set out annually on a *Stornoway* expedition. The capital of the Lews became one of the chief centres in Scotland for herring curing and export. More and more boats sailed here from the East Coast, while an increasing number of local craft made up the great fleet which assembled at Stornoway during the summer months. Steamers were chartered to take the cured herring to the mainland and the continent of Europe. *Lochboisdale* on South Uist developed into another important centre of the industry.

In 1868 James Methuen, one of the leading curers in Scotland, decided to make use of *Castlebay* on Barra. Within a few years it became a serious rival to Stornoway and Lochboisdale. It was said that its spacious natural harbour could not hold all the boats that tried to find berths. Some had to land their herring at *North Bay* and on the adjacent island of *Vatersay*. Right on until the first world war these three Hebridean centres of the herring industry held their own. There were bad seasons as well as good. During the summer months, fishermen, fishbuyers and fishworkers from many parts of Britain and from abroad, thronged the landing stages and curing yards. It was a cosmopolitan crowd. Fortunes were made and lost. Herring fishing and curing has always been a gamble.

Since the second world war Stornoway has remained one of the leading herring ports in this country, but landings in other places in the Hebrides have been insignificant. In recent years, to avoid dealing with big landings of herring at Stornoway, boats are often diverted to ports on the mainland where the fish can be immediately put on to lorries and rushed to curing or kippering yards in the North-East of Scotland.

It would be difficult to say just how many wonderful schemes have been drawn up to improve the Hebridean fisheries, not always for the benefit of the fishermen, but for the shareholders. Some of these schemes have been more disinterested than others.

In 1918 the late Lord Leverhulme spent vast sums of money on building piers, stores, curing stations, including a whaling station, and placing buoys and beacons in the Sound of Harris. A model village arose at Obbe, renamed *Leverburgh*. The whole thing proved a failure, like most of the many other schemes in the past two hundred years.

Very little inshore fishing, with the exception of small lines, is now carried on in the Outer Islands. Until the second world war there was no market. Prior to the first world war ling were caught in large quantities by big sailing boats and often sold as low as 6d per ling. Under such conditions it was impossible for the Hebridean fishermen to show much initiative. On the island of *Barra* inshore fishing is practically extinct from the commercial point of view. The *Eriskay* men are still doing their best to wrest a living from the sea, but as elsewhere in the Highlands and Islands they need larger and better boats. About ten years ago there were constant complaints that the fishing grounds were being depleted by English trawlers, and that the Minch must be closed to all vessels using this method of fishing. Actually, seine-netting is an even greater menace to the depletion of the stocks of fish.

There is not much prospect of any real development in the sea fisheries of the Highlands and Islands until better, cheaper and quicker transport facilities are obtained, especially for lobsters. In many instances fishermen need instruction in modern methods of fishing. It is possible that, if they were allowed a little more freedom of action, these men might yet be able to solve their own problems.

All round the North-West Coast, and on the Islands, there are young men who would like to become fishermen, but who, at the moment, find no alternative but to leave their homes and seek a living in more remunerative occupations.

* * * * * * *

The Fishery District of Campbeltown, which covers the much indented coast line from the Mull of Kintyre in the south to the Firth of Lorn in the north, with the islands of *Islay, Jura, Colonsay, Gigha,* etc., can be dealt with in a few lines. The only places where fishing has ever been of any commercial importance are *Campbeltown* itself and *Carradale* on Kilbrennan Sound. At these two ports ring-net boats land herring. The landings of white-fish by seine-net vessels at Campbeltown increased from 6,654 cwts. in 1938 to 20,313 cwts. in 1948. Shell fish are fairly profitable in this district.

The herring fisheries on the Firth of Clyde and Loch Fyne form a group by themselves and have been carried on since the Middle Ages. French vessels caught herring in these waters long before Scottish boats began to engage in fishing on a commercial basis. During the eighteenth century, buyers and curers came from many parts of Scotland and England. Most of the catch was sent to *Greenock* and other Clyde ports by fast sailing vessels. Drift-nets were used before 1830 for taking herring on the Firth of Clyde and adjacent lochs. About that date a special type of seine — known as a "ring-net" — worked by two boats, was introduced. This method of fishing superseded drift-nets. At first the change over to ring-nets aroused violent opposition. After interminable litigation the passing of the Sea Fisheries Act in 1868 allowed any sort of net to be used for herring. Even after this there were further protests that ring-netting had ruined the herring fisheries on Loch Fyne.

Greenock's association with herring goes back to the twelfth century. During the seventeenth century the port grew rich from cured herring. It was with good reason that the ancient motto of the burgh was "May herring swim which trade maintains." Large tracts of land were enclosed as curing yards and barrel factories. Most of the herring was exported to the West Indies. This trade began to decline when slavery in the British Colonies was abolished in 1833. Until the second-world war a considerable amount of herring was still landed at Greenock and *Gourock,* but in recent years the trade has declined.

Whale fishing was also carried on during the first years of the nineteenth century. Glasgow got its supplies of white fish from Greenock at this same period.

Rothesay on the Isle of Bute has been another important centre of the ring-net herring fisheries for a long period. *Saltcoats* was once a prosperous fishing port, but has long since declined.

Both white fish and herring were plentiful off *Ayr* in the eighteenth century. More than three thousand persons were employed in the herring trade at Ayr in 1780. The subsquent history of this port has been checkered. At the present time it is used as a base by many seine-net boats from the East Coast during the winter months, with the result that there has been a great development of this method of fishing in the Ballantrae District, in which Ayr is situated.

Dunure, Maidens and *Girvan* each maintain a fleet of up-to-date motor vessels, engaged both in herring and white fishing. *Ballantrae* was frequented by herring boats as far back as 1680. During the eighteenth century boats and busses gathered in Loch Ryan from every quarter to take part in the then prolific herring fisheries. *Stranraer* grew wealthy, and there was employment for everybody. By 1845 the herring shoals vanished from Loch Ryan, and Stranraer ceased to be an important fishing centre. The oyster beds in Loch Ryan have been famous for hundreds of years. To-day they are only worked on a small scale. None of the once fairly prosperous fishing villages in the south west corner of Scotland have gone forward, but *Portpatrick* is by no means dead. At *Port Logan, Sandhead,*

Glenluce, Port William, and *Isle of Whithorn* only a few boats remain. Lobsters are caught and there is a certain amount of line-fishing.

When Daniel Defoe wrote his *Tour of Great Britain*, published in 1724, he confessed that he could "discover no genius in the people of Wigtownshire for sea affairs in any kind." At the close of the eighteenth century, a minister whose parish was situated on the Solway Firth, wrote that "the inhabitants never think of profiting by the blessings which Providence has put into their power." The *Third Report of the British Fisheries* (1785) attributed the absence of any enthusiasm for sea fishing on this coast far more to the profits which could be made by smuggling than by any lack of fish. At no time do the fisheries of the shires of Kirkcudbright and Dumfries appear to have been exploited to any profit worth mentioning. *Annan* is the only port worth mentioning. As far back as 1790 many of its inhabitants were employed in the fisheries. Salmon, white fish and prawns were landed. About 1858 English fishermen from Morecambe settled at Annan, bringing with them a type of boat that is still used on the Solway Firth (see p. 108).

CHAPTER VII.

METHODS OF FISHING—TRAWLING, DRIFT-NET, SEINE-NET, Etc.

At the present time the chief methods of fishing used by Scottish fishermen are: *deep-sea trawling, great-lining* for white fish; *drift-net fishing* for herring; and *seine netting* for white fish.* Lobsters and crabs are captured in creels; salmon are taken with fixed nets.

(1) *TRAWLING.*

Before the second world war about 85 per cent. of the white fish landed in Scottish ports came from steam trawlers. The most important species taken are cod, haddock, plaice and hake. Other fish include whiting, halibut, turbot, lemon sole, skate and ling.

It was not until 1882 that trawling was started in this country. In that year a beginning was made at Aberdeen. As has been stated already, it aroused great indignation among the local fishermen. Most of the first steam trawlers were old paddle-tugs, converted for fishing, and bought from Sunderland, Scarborough and other English ports. During the next twenty years, steam gradually replaced sail. Eventually Aberdeen became the third trawling port in Great Britain.

Trawling is now carried on by vessels working from Aberdeen, Leith, Granton and Dundee. As will be seen from the following tables, *Aberdeen* is by far the most important centre of the white fish industry. It ranks next to Hull and Grimsby, both as to the total amount and the value of the catch. *Leith* and *Granton* come next in order. Some of their trawlers work on the West Coast and land their catches at *Oban* and *Ayr.* There are only seven vessels working from *Dundee.*

* * * * * * *

---

*Percentage to Total White-fish catch by each method of fishing:—

	Trawl	*Seine Net*	*Great Line*	*Small & Hand Lines*	*Other*
1938	75.7	10.4	7.2	6.1	0.6
1948	63.3	26.6	8.5	1.2	0.4

TRAWLERS AT ABERDEEN.

TRAWLERS AT ABERDEEN.

An "otter-trawl" is a net from 70 to about 120 feet across the mouth and about 110 feet from the mouth to the "cod-end." It consists of three parts: (1) the wings, (2) the "belly," (3) the "cod-end." The netting is of coarse hemp, the mesh increasing from about 1 inch at the cod-end to about 3 inches near the mouth. The mouth of the net is kept open by two wooden "otter-boards" (clamped with an iron shoe), attached to the net and to the warps by which the net is towed by chains and shackles, in such a way that the pressure of the water causes them to keep

HAULING-IN A TRAWL-NET.

apart. The otter-boards measure about 11 feet by 4 feet 6 inches. The steel warps may be from three hundred to more than a thousand fathoms long—about three times as long as the depth of water in which the trawl is shot. Each board is attached to the mouth of the net by a separate warp. The upper edge of the mouth of the net is attached to a strong rope (the "head-rope"). The lower edge is made fast to a "foot-rope." The latter is longer than the former and makes up the "bosom" of the net. Sometimes when being drawn over rough ground the foot-rope is attached to large wooden rollers, called "bobbins."

A trawl-net is "shot" every five or six hours. The labour is continuous. The operation of hauling the nets is roughly as follows. One man stands at the steam-winch. The rest of the crew are stationed on the side, waiting while the steel warp is slowly wound round the two drums. At last the two otter boards come up over the bulwarks. They are secured close to the "gallowses" (steel framework), two fore and two aft. Then comes the foot-rope and lastly the net itself. A rope is passed round the cod-end, which is hauled up by means of a block until it is above the "pounds," i.e. the boards dividing the foredeck. One of the crew gets underneath the net and unties the "cod-line" by which the bottom is secured. Down falls a shower of fish on to the deck. The cod-end is tied up again and the gear shot once more. When this is done the crew carry on with gutting the fish. After it has been washed and sorted, it is put in the baskets and passed down through the hatch into the hold, where it is laid on shelves between ice. The work goes on in the same manner until the vessel proceeds back to her port. It is only then that the crew can get a rest from their labour.

Aberdeen trawlers are usually classified as "Long trippers" and "Scratchers." The former work off Iceland, the Faroes, the Orkneys and Shetland, or off the North-West Coast. In recent years a few have ventured as far off as the Barents Sea and Bear Island. The latter mostly fish off the East Coast, on the North Sea grounds. They land their catches several times a week.* Most of the Scottish trawlers are old and obsolete vessels.† They are unable to

---

*Quantities and percentages of landings from chief fishing regions in 1938 and 1948:—

Quantity (1000 cwt.)	Total	North Sea	West of Scotland	Faroe	Iceland	Barents Sea, Bear Island, & White Sea	Other Grounds
1938	2,504.2	1,885.7	232.1	242.2	81.6	—	62.7
1948	3,356.7	2,079.3	387.5	352.5	316.1	64.3	156.9
Per Cent.							
1938	100.0	75.3	9.3	9.7	3.2	—	2.5
1948	100.0	62.0	11.5	10.5	9.4	1.9	4.7

† *Age*	*Leith*	*Dundee*	*Aberdeen*	*Peterhead*
Under 10 years	2	—	7	—
10-14	1	—	2	—
15-19	11	—	12	—
20-24	—	—	3	—
25 and over	45	7	169	2
Total	59	7	193	2

compete with the large and up-to-date vessels belonging to Hull and Grimsby.

Before 1939, about 74 per cent. of the total amount of trawled fish landed in Scotland was marketed at Aberdeen. The number of men then regularly employed in Scottish steam trawlers was as follows:

Aberdeen	2718
Leith and Granton	595
Dundee	67
Total	3380

A certain number of men were employed in trawlers when not engaged in the herring fisheries. During the years immediately after the first world war, when the export of cured herring greatly declined, hundreds of men from the Moray Firth coast migrated to Aberdeen or even to English ports to find jobs in trawlers. The only alternative was the dole. But the trawling industry itself was in an unsettled state, due to continual increase in running expenses and uncertain markets.

In 1939 there were 346 steam trawlers registered in Scotland and about 1,400 registered in England and Wales. Even ten years ago most of the Scottish vessels were obselete and should have been scrapped. The future of the white-fish trade in Aberdeen was causing grave anxiety. It was obvious that unless drastic measures were taken, the only big trawling port in Scotland would decline. With the outbreak of war the whole situation changed. Regulations on fishing were imposed that often suggested that those responsible for them may have had little experience of the conditions of catching or marketing fish. The Scottish white fish trade was reduced to a state of chaos. Even to-day the situation is confused, and it is not easy to say what is to be the future of trawling in Scotland, granted that the landings and profits are higher than they were ten years ago.

* * * * * * *

The trawling industry is the most highly organised branch of the sea fisheries. The majority of vessels are owned by companies. Small groups of owners are still characteristic of Aberdeen, whereas in England, the tendency is all for the merging of companies into combines.

In 1936, the Sea Fish Commission for the United Kingdom published an exhaustive Report, which gave official approval to group ownership for economic reasons. "Solidarity of outlook and agreed course of action" were brought forward as other advantages of grouping the white-fish industry into big companies. There was a certain amount of truth in the statement that these two factors "are always most difficult of achievement by voluntary measures where there is a large number of voting units."

In Scotland, the fishing industry has been handicapped for many years by its lack of "solidarity of outlook and of agreed course of action." For this reason alone it has been unable to compete with England. Nevertheless it must be stressed that the group ownership in the form of large companies and combines has transformed the English white fish industry into a typical " big business," with all the disadvantages involved by the suppression of individual effort and ownership. The only hope for Scotland would seem to be in the development of co-operative methods among fishermen and other persons engaged in the fish trade. Otherwise, sooner or later, our trawlers will be bought up by English combines, and no longer shall we be able to call our fisheries our own. They will be in the hands of foreigners.

In Scottish trawlers, skippers and mates are paid a share of the net earnings. The deck and engine-room ratings are paid weekly wages. In addition they receive a share of the net earnings of the voyage, should these exceed a recognised amount, together with certain perquisites. Aberdeen trawler crews have to pay for their food out of their wages.

Although the trawlers cannot offer the same comfortable conditions as those found in most of the vessels working from the larger English ports, it can be said that, in some ways, there is a happier spirit in Scottish trawlers, just because the "family spirit" has persisted to a large degree. In many of the Aberdeen trawlers, practically all the crew are natives of the same port or district. In a Hull or Grimsby vessel the crew may be made up of men drawn from all parts of England.

Trawler owners and fishermen have their Trade Unions, similar to those found in all other forms of modern industrial life. These Unions have helped to bring about improvements in the living conditions at sea, also to settle grievances between owners and crews. During the last war, and since, the Trawler Owners' Associations and Fishermens' Unions have engaged in protracted negotiations with the Ministry of Labour and National Service, concerning the regulation ot wages and working conditions in general.

Life in a modern steam trawler is hard enough. Long hours of work, combined with the discomfort of cold and wet, are inevitable features of the life. Trips of ten days or a fortnight from Aberdeen to Iceland or the Faroes, or nearer waters, are relieved with little more than a couple of days ashore, unless the vessel has to be laid up for a refit, or there is a strike among the fishermen. The trawlerman is seldom at home for more than two nights on end. Not a few of the Aberdeen crews still have their homes on the Moray Firth coast.

The Scottish trawling industry has been built up in the past seventy years by supplying a high quality of fish, rather than by quantity. It has been said that the fish landed at Aberdeen is the *best* put on the markets of any port in Britain. This is mainly due to it being caught in less remote waters. The age and size of the average Scottish steam trawler makes it impossible for her to venture more than a given distance. This high quality of fish goes with the disadvantage of far smaller quantities landed, which, in the long run, is an economic loss. Before the last war the growth of the fish and chip shops had created a demand for cheap fish—something which the Scottish trawlers could not supply in sufficient quantites. The demand was so great that even English ports could not always meet it. Fish had to be imported from Norway and Denmark.

Landings of White Fish by British Trawlers in Scottish ports

	Total		Steam.		Motor.	
	1000 cwts.	£1000.	1000 cwts.	£1000.	1000 cwts.	£1000.
38	1,896.3	2,036.8	1,894.0	2,033.3	2.3	3.5
48	2,124.1	5,273.8	2,104.2	5,237.2	19.9	36.6

Quantity of proportion of Scottish trawl landings in Aberdeen

	Quantity 1000 cwts.	Value £1000.	Percentage of total quantity
38	1,437	1,571	76
48	1,441	3,372	68

British trawlers landing in Aberdeen

	Arrivals.	Number of trawler working at Aberdee
1938	13,025	320
1948	4,221	171

Average catch and gross earnings of Aberdeen trawlers

	Average Catch.	Average Earnings.
1938	24.8	25.7
1948	40.7	90.7

Landings by Leith District Trawlers at Leith, Granton, Oban a Ayr

		Leith & Granton.		Oban		Ayr.	
	Trawlers.	Arrivals.	1000 cwts.	Arrivals.	1000 cwts.	Arrivals.	1000 cw
1938	58	1,566	626	190	35	59	8
1948	60	2,311	392	21	5	27	9

Quantities and values of fish landed by Foreign vessels in Scotla

	Quantity (1000 cwts.)		Value £1C	
	Total.	Herring & Mackerel.	Total.	Herring & Macker
1938	117.7	0.48	118.3	0.02
1948	529.4	0.12	1,266.0	0.29

Foreign landings of all fish in Scottish ports

TOTAL	1938.	1000 cwts.	1948.
	117.7		529.4
Belgian	0.5		4.4
Danish	5.3		89.0
Dutch	—		—
Faroese	1.1		383.7
French	—		0.1
German	73.5		—
Icelandic	3.0		4.9
Norwegian	3.3		8.0
Polish	—		0.2
Swedish	31.0		39.1

(2) *GREAT-LINING.*

Until 1939 there were between twenty and thirty vessels, similar to steam trawlers, engaged in "great-lining" from Aberdeen. Their catches gradually declined, and by 1939 were reduced to less than one-third of those in 1921. Smaller vessels of the herring-drifter class carried on this method of fishing from Peterhead and some of the Fife ports.

Great-liners may shoot about 30 baskets of line, each containing 480 fathoms of line, with a snood or branch line and hook every 3 fathoms. This makes a total of 15 miles of line and more than 5,000 hooks. Even with the help of a steam line hauler it is a laborious job, added to which is the labour of baiting every hook!

This method of fishing began to recover after 1944, and by 1948 the number of vessels engaged in great-lining had risen from 9 to 22, all of them working from Aberdeen with satisfactory results. A certain number of East Coast drifter-liners and motor vessels have fished off the West Coast in recent years, generally landing their catches at Stornoway, Mallaig, Oban and Stranraer. Motor vessels of the Anstruther District have been fishing with great-lines in the Firth of Forth. Ling, halibut, torsk, cod and skate are among the species taken. In 1948 halibut proved the most remunerative; the total landings of 58,081 cwt. for last year realised £475,652.

(3) *DRIFT-NET FISHING.*

Herring and mackerel are pelagic fish and usually swim near the surface of the water. At certain times of the year they gather in shoals. The fish swim against long walls of finely meshed netting, and are caught by their gills. The nets are called "drift," because once they have been shot, the vessel drifts with the tide for three or four hours before the nets are hauled. A drifter may let out a fleet of nets more than a mile in length. Herring are measured by the "cran." One Scottish cran equals 3½ cwt., i.e. from 900 to 1000 herrings according to size. The baskets in which the fish are discharged hold one quarter of a cran.

There is not much difference in the manner of working drift-nets whether the vessel be steam, motor or sail. The usual time for beginning work is just about sunset. When the fishermen think that they have arrived on grounds where herring is likely to be taken, immediate preparations are made.* The nets have already been stowed in regular order in the hold. To prevent any danger of getting entangled while they are passing over the deck,

---

*Aeroplanes are now used in certain districts to locate shoals of herring.

a "bank board" is placed between the hatch and the top of the bulwark, over which they are hauled; a roller at the edge of the hold taking off the strain on them as they are drawn up from below. The warp, or "messenger rope," to which the nets are attached, is run out over a roller, called a "molgogger." Two men shoot the nets; the one taking charge of the corks, buoy-ropes ("stoppers") and buoys ("bows"); the other looking after the netting itself. Another man attends to the "seizings" of the nets as they come up on deck. He passes them forward to the mate, who makes them fast to the warp as it runs out over the molgogger. When all the fleet of nets has been paid out, fifteen to twenty fathoms more warp is let go as a "swing rope." The vessel is then brought round head to wind. A mizzen is usually set to keep the drifter in this position, and the foremast is lowered. Two white lights are placed to show that the vessel is fishing; the lower of the two indicating the actual direction of the nets. The watch is set, and the vessel drifts with the tide. In bad weather more swing-rope is needed, so that there may not be too great a drag on the nets.

When the nets are in the water the warp is occasionally hauled in as far as the first net to see if fish are about. After three or four hours the process of hauling begins. The warp, or "bush rope," is led through a block fixed on the bulwarks, near the capstan, and down into the rope-room, where one of the crew, usually the boy-cook, coils it down so as to be ready for running out when it is again wanted. One man, the "cast-off," disconnects the nets from the warp; two others take charge of the "bows" and seizings, and four more stand in the hold and shake out the fish from the nets. The "bows" are stowed away in the wings of the hold. Should there be a good catch, hauling may take several hours. As soon as the last of the nets has been brought on board the vessel proceeds back to port. The men draw out all the nets from the hold, shake out any fish that may still be entangled in the mesh, and pile the nets on either side of the deck. On arriving in port a sample of herring is taken up at once to the market by two of the crew, unless the drifter should be working for some particular curing-firm, in which case the fish is landed at once, close to the gutting-sheds. In the old sailing days, long before radio was ever dreamed of, homer pigeons were sometimes carried on board, and released after the nets were hauled. Thus those on shore got word of the amount of the catch.

Drift-nets need constant attention and frequent mending, especially in these days when a new net costs £14. Every Saturday Scottish fishermen "bark" their nets by

HAULING DRIFT-NETS.

immersing them for two or three minutes in a strong solution of tanning and boiling water. The nets are then laid out to dry until Monday morning.

* * * * * * *

Herring fisheries have always been carried on much more off Scotland than off England and Wales. As has been stated already, it was not until early in the last century that the herring industry became of any real commercial value to the Scottish nation. Until then, the only purely Scottish herring fisheries were those on the Firth of Clyde. Elsewhere foreign vessels caught herring. The industry went on developing right through the last century, and reached its utmost prosperity between 1900 and 1910. After the first world war the herring fisheries suffered a severe setback. There was no longer the same demand for cured herring abroad. Prices dropped, and the number of persons employed, both at sea and ashore, decreased at an alarming rate. There was a rapid deterioration of vessels and gear.

The herring fisheries have their definite localities and regular seasons. Until about ten years ago the fishing started off the West Coast of Scotland in May and continued round the East Coast until December. Scottish drifters ended their fisheries at the close of the East Anglian season in November. There was also an important winter fishing off the North-West Coast and in the Firth of Forth. The Firth of Clyde and Loch Fyne fisheries went on throughout the year, whenever shoals of herring appeared. Ring-nets have always been the favourite gear employed on the Firth of Clyde and Loch Fyne. They are worked by two boats at the same time.*

Before 1939 the chief ports in Scotland where herring was landed were *Lerwick* (Shetland), *Stronsay* (Orkney), *Stornoway* (Lewis), *Castlebay* (Barra), *Mallaig, Wick, Fraserburgh* and *Peterhead.* Other ports on the mainland of Scotland, which had curing yards until early in the present century gradually declined after steam replaced sail. Before that it was necessary to have curing yards in every port, large or small, within access of the regular fishing grounds.

Scottish drifters also fished from many English ports during the late summer and autumn, including *North Shields, Hartlepool, Whitby, Scarborough, Grimsby, Yarmouth* and *Lowestoft.* During the East Anglian autumn season, Scottish vessels were usually in excess of English drifters†

* * * * * * *

---

*A vivid and detailed description of ring-net fishing on Loch Fyne is given in *Men and Herring* by Naomi Mitchison and Denis Macintosh. (Serif Books, 1949.)

†These statistics show the decrease in number of personnel connected with the Scottish herring fisheries between the two world wars:—

	1913	1937
Fishermen (approximate)	20.500	15,000
Gutters and packers	16,269	6,726
Coopers	3,116	1,508
Fish curers	2,662	1,012

During the first years of the last war the herring fisheries, as was inevitable, were much curtailed. A limited number of Scottish drifters—about half the total number—took part in the East Anglian fishing in the autumn of 1939. The Scottish Herring Producer's Association selected boats by ballot. In 1940 the Ministry of Food took over all herring which could not be sold for the home market. Profits made on the sale of herring were distributed as a bonus to all fishermen landing herring for which 30s a cran was paid. The Ministry and the Scottish Home Department reserved the right to restrict herring fishing when there were excessive landings. Many other regulations were enforced. During the summer seasons of 1942 and 1943 curing was allowed to be carried on at Fraserburgh, Buckie and Wick, but on a very small scale; the fishermen being paid from 60s to 91s per cran. By 1944 herring was landed in other ports, and further regulations of fishing were enforced by the Ministry of Food. Owing to occasional very heavy catches and limited transport available, ports had to be closed again and again that year. Fraserburgh remained the chief centre of the fishing. Shortage of labour and barrels hampered herring curing in 1945, and a restriction was placed on the number of nets used by drifters. In the autumn of this year fishing was resumed off East Anglia. In 1946 the Herring Industry Board, in conjunction with the Ministry of Food, took over the production and export of herring. During the summer curing was carried on at Fraserburgh, Peterhead, Wick, Buckie, Stornoway and in Shetland. Disputes between buyers and fishermen frequently interrupted fishing.

In the autumn of 1946 203 Scottish steam-drifters and 57 motor vessels took part in the East Anglian fisheries, which were marked by several strikes by fishermen, as well as by male and female fish workers; the former claiming full seamen's food rations; the latter higher wages. By the summer of 1947 the maximum price for herring was raised to 89s 10d per cran. A price of 55s per cran was decided on for curing. The Herring Industry Board agreed to take over the whole cure on a co-operative basis. The Ministry of Food offered to handle most of the surplus of herring at a price of 30s per cran for reduction to oil and meal. At first the majority of fishermen were not enthusiastic about this scheme. Castlebay was re-opened for the first time since 1939, but the fishing from Barra was not so profitable as from Lerwick and Wick. In these two ports most of the herring was processed. In the autumn of 1947 212 Scottish steam-drifters and 83 motor vessels engaged in the East Anglian fisheries. Although many nets were lost, it was a fairly successful season.

In 1948 the North West Coast herring fisheries were above the average. During the summer and autumn fishings the maximum price remained at 89s 10d per cran, with an agreed price for curing and klondyking at 60s per cran, and 35s for processing for oil and meal. Once again the Herring Industry Board offered to buy the whole cure. The summer fishings at Stornoway and in the Shetlands were successful, but poor on the East Coast. Some 113 motor drifters besides 191 steam drifters from Scottish ports were working from Yarmouth and Lowestoft in the autumn. The season was fairly profitable both to fishermen and processors, but there was a fall in sales for the home markets.

* * * * * * *

It is possible that one reason why the Scottish drifter fishermen may have failed to hold their own is their strong individualism and inability to act co-operatively. The crews of English drifters are paid wages. Practically all the vessels are owned by companies. Their owners provide the nets and gear. The cost of food is deducted before wages are paid. But the Scottish fishermen still own most of their drifters, or, to be more correct, they are the nominal owners. In many cases during the lean years after the first world war, drifters and shore property had to be transferred to wives or other persons on shore to enable the men to draw the dole. In England, practically all herring fishermen are concentrated in a few large ports. They are backed up by companies and have the advantage of group-ownership of vessels. This means unlimited capital. Most of the Scottish drifter crews live in widely scattered areas on the East Coast from Berwick to the Pentland Firth or in Shetland. To the bureaucratic mind this must be very irritating. There are already signs that those in high places, far away in the south of England, who control the destinies of the Scottish fishermen, are trying to concentrate them in a few large ports for economic reasons. Meanwhile, the men, to a large extent, have to rely on themselves unless they fall back on loans from merchants or other persons with money behind them, or on the State as a last resort. The average Scottish fisherman is still in the unhappy—or happy—position of a small shopkeeper. It is hard for him to have a compete with "Big Business!"

The 1932 *Report of the Economic Advisory Council on the Fishing Industry* thus summed up the situation as it was seventeen years ago:

> "In the main each Scottish boat stands by itself, and there is no pooling of results and no possibility of a loss on one boat being balanced by the success of others, as in the case of a company owning a number of vessels. This is mitigated to some extent by the fact that a small number of individuals, mostly on shore, have a share in several boats. The men are also extremely conservative. They are prejudiced against change. Their spirit of independence is fostered by the organisation of the industry."

Most of these more or less independent drifters carry crews of nine or ten men, the majority of whom are related to each other. In the smaller motor vessels only five or six men form the crew. The fireman, engineer and cook (formerly always a boy, but in these times with fewer and fewer boys going to sea, often an elderly man) are paid wages. The other men receive certain shares in the earnings of their drifter. But it is typical of the individualism of the Scottish fishemen, even in 1949, that there should still be considerable differences in details of remuneration in different ports or Fishing Districts. As the cost of new vessels is now double what it was before 1939* and the prices of nets† and all other gear has risen accordingly, the financial strain on maintaining a steam or motor drifter is becoming more and more acute.

By 1939 the condition of the Scottish herring fleet was alarming enough: to-day it is worse. The number of

*An average size dual-purpose motor vessel costs from £8,000 to £10,000.

†Now £14 each.

vessels had decreased from 884 in 1913 to 402 in 1938. In 1948 there were only 228 steam-drifters left in Scotland. Most of these are old and unseaworthy. No new steam drifters have been built since 1932. Of the total of 228 vessels 155 are over thirty years old, and only five less than twenty years old. They are distributed as follows:

Peterhead	88
Buckie	48
Fraserburgh	35
Banff	22
Aberdeen	13
Stornoway	13
Findhorn	2
Anstruther	3
Shetland	3
Eyemouth	1
Total	228

In 1934 it was discovered by the Sea Fish Commission that 357 out of 430 drifters whose accounts had been investigated had an average debt of well over £580—this money being owed to the fish salesmen. There are many drifters in 1948 which are in much the same financial straits.

Against all this it must be stated that the dwindling fleet of steam drifters is gradually being superseded by modern motor vessels. In 1948 there were 460 motor vessels chiefly used for herring fishing. That year 99 motor vessels of 45 feet and over were built at a total cost of £760,733; 75 vessels of the same dimensions in 1947 and 28 in 1946. The fleet has also been increased by the addition of a large number of Admiralty-built diesel-motor vessels (M.F.Vs.), originally used by the Navy, but since allocated to fishermen.

* * * * * * *

Herring, after they have been sold on landing, are re-sold as "fresh herring," or kippered, canned or cured. The larger part of fresh herring and kippers are for home markets. Until 1914 there was an almost insatiable demand for cured herring in Russia, Germany and many other countries in the continent of Europe. A certain amount was exported to North America. After the first world war the export of cured herring declined. Many factors contributed to this: Russia, Holland and later on, Germany developed their own herring fisheries. Other nations found that cheap canned salmon was more palatable than salt herring. The demand for the latter dropped at an alarming rate.*

Then in 1940 the number of barrels exported from Scotland dropped to 9,209, of which 5,825 went to Sweden. Then, until 1945 there were no further direct exports of cured herring from Scotland, when 88,016 barrels were dispatched—49,638 to Belgium. In 1948 the amount had risen

LANDING HERRING AT LERWICK.

to 169,937½ barrels of cured herring and 40,908 barrels of cured ungutted herring, the greater part of which went to Germany.

---

*			
1907 ...	2,578,268	barrels cured in	Scotland.
1915 ...	175,469	,,	,,
1924 ...	1,722,759	,,	,,
1935 ...	932,856	,,	,,
1937 ...	612,942	,,	,,

Before 1914 Scotland had almost a monopoly of the cured herring trade, but by 1937 the number of barrels cured in Germany had risen to 1,001,500, and a similar increase took place in Holland and Norway. Despite frequent appeals to the British public to "Eat More Fish," there was a drop of 45 per cent. in the home consumption of this herring in the twenty years previous to the second world war. Even more startling is the fact that about 25 per cent. of the total amount of herring landed in Britain came from Norway—the result of a trade agreement.

To-day it is difficult to picture the incredible prosperity of the Scottish herring fisheries before 1914. On an average half a million crans were landed every year. About three quarters of this amount was pickled in brine and exported in barrels to most parts of Europe. About 6 per cent. of the total was made into red herrings. There were markets for it in the Mediterranean countries, even in Africa. By 1934 matters had reached such a pass that there were far too many drifters. An "orderly contraction" of the fleet was started. The Herring Board scrapped as many vessels as possible, or sold them to other nations, not realising, perhaps, that one of these customers would be at war with us five years later. As Mr Michael Graham remarks in "*The Fish Gate*" (p. 94.)

> "It was part of a great effort, but all the care and thought and disinterested planning of the various Commissions, all the meticulous drafting and skilful pilotage through the House that followed, amounted only to this, that after losing part of the market, we wrung our hands, and tried to throw valuable ships and men away too. That is what we were like in the '30's."

* * * * * * *

It is difficult, if not impossible to prophesy, what is to be the future of the Scottish herring industry—nobody can tell. The supply of herring is far greater than the present demand. "By reason of the abundance of the herring and its extreme perishability, methods of preservation are of prime importance to the industry, and the decline of pickle curing on which the industry has relied in the past has been the most adverse result of the two world wars. Apart from curing, the principal means of preservation in Scotland are kippering and canning, but freezing is expanding. Only small quantities are converted in Scotland into bloaters, red herring or bücklinge. A new method of dry-curing herring for export to tropical countries is in process of development by the Herring Industry Board who are also making rapid progress with plans for the manufacture of herring oil and meal on an extended scale."

This is how the Scottish Home Department sums up the situation in the 1939-1948 *Report on the Fisheries of Scotland* (p. 47).

The establishment of quick-freezing plants on a larger scale, and improved transport facilities could double the home consumption of fresh herrings. Freezing plants would also assure a regular supply of kippers throughout the year. The shortage of timber makes it difficult to obtain enough barrels for exporting cured herring. So new methods of packing must be devised. There is a world shortage of fats and edible oils. Herring can be also transformed into fish-meal.

The Herring Board has all sorts of schemes for the development of the fisheries, but as Mr A. C. Hardy remarks in *Seafood Ships* (p. 80). "The Board's task is not an easy one because of the very conservative nature of the herring industry. It aims at converting a casual hit and miss, badly organised, speculative employment into a scientifically controlled source of national wealth and food." To the average Scots fisherman the prospect would seem to be a state-owned herring fleet and herring industry. Would Scots fishermen like having their vessels, gear, and all else "Nationalised?" How much would they lose or gain in the long run if the herring, and probably the white fisheries, were directed and controlled from London? If the in many ways admirable dreams of the Herring Board come true, how much will Scotland benefit by the herring landed by her own fishermen in her own ports? What is certain is that increased mechanisation of the industry and a reduction of the fleet would mean an even greater reduction in man-power. There would be fewer fishermen and fish-workers required.

STATISTICS OF HERRING FISHERIES.

Number of Scottish fishing vessels, and total amount of landings and value (£ thousand) in East Anglian herring fishing (1939 and 1948)—

	1938	1948
VESSELS		
Total	444	304
Steam	378	191
Motor	66	113
LANDINGS		
Quantity (1000 cwts.)	892	952
Steam	806	637
Motor	85	315
VALUE		
(£1000)	239	946
Steam	215	627
Motor	24	319

Herring landed by Scottish vessels in other English, Irish and Manx fisheries (1938 and 1948)—

	Total.		Other English			Irish & Isle of Man		
	1000 cwts.	£1000.	Vessels.	1000 cwts.	£1000.	Vessels.	1000 cwts.	£1000
1938	39.5	12.5	20	11.4	3.7	27	28.1	8.7
1948	194.2	203.9	161	129.5	131.3	104	64.7	72.6

All the vessels engaged in 1948 were motor boats, except 2 steam drifters landing at North Shields and Grimsby.

Landings of herring by British vessels in Scotland and number of vessels and fishermen engaged in 1938 and 1948—

	Vessels.			Herring Landings.		
					Average price per cwt.	
	Steam.	Motor.	Fishermen.	1000 cwts.	S	D
1938	402	568	6,734	2,801	7	7
1948	228	460	5,148	2,913	21	2

Landings of herring by method of capture in 1938 and 1948—

	Total.	Drifters. Steam.	Drifters. Motor.	Sail.	Trawlers.	Ring-net.	Motor-seiners.
938	2,800.6	1,578.0	503.0	3.7	120.4	595.4	—
948	2,913.2	1,278.2	801.1	0.7	171.9	660.6	0.7

Ring-Net catches of herring in 1938 and 1948—

	All Scotland.		Forth Area.		Clyde Area.		Rest of West Coast.	
	1000 cwts.	£1000.	1000 cwts	£1000.	1000 cwts.	£1000	1000 cwts.	£1000
938	595	199	214	75	352	110	28	14
948	661	733	7	8	263	388	289	336

Herring landed in Firth of Clyde in 1938 and 1948—

	1000 cwts.	Value £1000.	Average price per cwt.
1938	352	110	6s 3d
1948	363	388	21s 3d

Herring landed in the Firth of Forth in 1938 and 1948—

	1000 cwts.	£1000.	Average price per cwt.
1938	373	132	7s 1d
1948	21	25	24s 2d

Herring landed in Shetland (April to September) in 1938 and 1948—

	1000 cwts.	£1000.	Average price per cwt.
1938	600	225	7s 6d
1948	498	421	16s 11d

Herring landed on North-West Coasts, according to season, 1938 and 1948—

	January to March.		April to September.		October to December.	
	1000 cwts.	Average price.	1000 cwts.	Average price.	1000 cwts.	Average price
938	37	7s 7d	238	11s 0d	56	7s 5d
948	180	24s 2d	353	20s 0d	220	23s 2d

Herring landed on East Coast from April to September 1938 and 1948—

	1000 cwts.	£1000.	Average price per cwt.
1938	1,050	387	7s 4d
1948	1,217	1,554	25s 6d

Landings of herring by Scottish vessels in England, Northern Ireland and the Isle of Man in 1938 and 1948—

	Total.		Steam.		Motor.	
	1000 cwts.	£1000.	1000 cwts.	£1000.	1000 cwts.	£1000.
1938	931.3	251.8	811.1	217.0	120.2	34.8
1948	1,146.2	1,150.1	644.4	634.6	501.9	515.5

Disposal of Scottish herring in 1938 and 1948—

	Total landed.	Fresh to Home markets.	Exported Fresh (Klondyked).	Kippered.	Bloaters, Reds, etc.	Canned.	Pickled.
1938	2,801.1	472.0	366.0	522.1	3.9	117.5	1,319.6
1948	3,089.8	909.7	332.0	1,108.8	2.6	152.4	584.3

Number and Earnings of Gutters and Packers, etc. (1938 and 1948)—

	Women gutters, packers, kipperers, etc.	Earnings of Gutters and Packers. Scottish Fishings.		East Anglian Fishing.	
		Total. £	Average.	Total. £	Average. £
1938	6,347	52,491	16	37,542	17
1948	4,764	46,170	46	33,728	58

Scottish coopers employed and number of whole and half barrels made (1938 and 1948)—

	Coopers.	Barrels.	½ Barrels.
1938	919	264,895	388,447
1948	376	283,519	58,571

(3) *INSHORE FISHING (SEINE-NETS AND LINES.)*

Unlike the trawler and drifter fishermen who work at a considerable distance from land, according to circumstances, the inshore fishermen confine their labour to within a few miles of the coast. Until about the middle of the last century, all Scottish fishermen were "inshore" in the literal meaning of the word. Even to-day the inshore fisheries of this country are of much greater importance than those of England. In 1938 the Scottish inshore catch of white fish amounted to about 15 per cent. of the total landings. For England and Wales only 1 per cent. came from inshore fishing vessels. To-day the word "inshore" is hardly applicable in the case of the larger motor-vessels, because many of them work with seine-nets at a great distance from their home ports, and in some cases are away for several weeks. The almost complete disappearance of inshore fishermen around England and Wales, due to the concentration of the industry in a few large centres, may yet happen to a lesser degree in Scotland within ten or twenty years, unless practical measures are enforced to prevent it.

Inshore fishermen take herring and mackerel besides most of the same species of white-fish landed by deep-sea trawlers and great-liners. On some parts of the coast inshore fishing is combined with the catching of shell fish.

Since about 1921, both long and hand-lines* have been superseded by the Danish seine-net as the usual means of capture, except in the small open boats which survive in a few ports on the East Coast and in many districts of the West Highlands Drift and ring nets are used for herring and mackerel. Staked nets are still found in some places. Unlike Englishmen, Scottish inshore fishermen have seldom used either a beam or otter-trawl.

It is not easy to give accurate figures of the number of inshore fishermen in Scotland at the present time. Many of them, especially on the North-West Coast and in the Islands, only revert to it at certain seasons of the year. They are *Crofter-Fishermen*. According to the official Reports, there were 4,067 crofter-fishermen in 1938 and 3,733 in 1948. About 1936 there were reckoned to be approximately 10,076 inshore fishermen in this country, but the numbers must have greatly declined since then. The following figures show the number of men employed in sail and motor-boats in 1913 and 1937—a period of a quarter of a century.

	Sail.	Motor.
1913	21,934	2,246
1937	3,455	8,213

*Two kinds of *hand-lines*—haddock and cod—were in general use by Scottish inshore-fishermen. Haddock lines consisted of from 800 to 1000 hooks, on snoods of 14 inches, 2½ feet apart. Mussels and lugworms were used as bait. Cod lines had about 80 snoods. 5 feet long and 2½ feet apart. Herring and small haddock were used as bait. Cod lines were also employed for ling, skate, halibut and turbot.

Each baited line was laid out carefully, in a "scull," i.e. a wooden tray of special design. Freshly plucked grass was spread between the snoods so that they could run out clear when the line was shot. The baiting of lines is now an almost forgotten art on the East Coast.

Great-lines were arranged in baskets, with the baited hooks stuck into the edge of the wicker-work.

The inshore fisheries of Scotland can be divided into those of the East and North Coasts (including the Orkneys and Shetland), and the West Coast. The fundamental difference between them is that in the former fishing is generally

INSHORE FISHING BOATS, PORT SETON.

a whole-time occupation; in the latter, except on the Firth of Clyde, the majority of the men only regard fishing as a part-time job.

(a) *East Coast.*

There are no more enterprising fishermen anywhere in the British Isles than those on the East Coast of Scotland and between Berwick-on-Tweed and the Shetland Islands. Largely through their own initiative, and hitherto with little or no outside help, they have managed to earn a reasonable livelihood from inshore fishing. Some Districts are more prosperous than others, some are declining, others are going ahead. The following table shows the landings of white fish by British seine-net vessels in Scottish Fishery Districts in 1938 and 1948.

	1938		1948	
	cwts.	£	cwts.	£
Eyemouth	3,216	3,741	48,715	81,344
Leith	9,980	15,852	11,838	36,344
Anstruther	51	66	16,507	33,426
Montrose	18,739	20,309	27,710	75,387
Stonehaven	2,356	2,811	3,373	8,840
Aberdeen	7,241	9,686	54,860	126,251
Peterhead	2,726	5,306	128,614	244,039
Fraserburgh	3,588	10,200	112,009	224,940
Banff	24,852	42,928	43,113	101,793
Buckie	5,958	10,386	56,763	140,444
Findhorn	102,432	128,151	74,618	203,658
Helmsdale	13,950	16,607	13,182	42,726
Lybster	2,611	4,481	4,662	15,091
Wick	22,477	33,457	94,544	249,264
Shetland	629	727	48,901	110,664
Fort William	2,159	1,907	74,003	209,437
Campbeltown	6,654	7,010	20,313	38,530
Inverary	46	105	3,312	8,009
Rothesay	325	776	1,023	3,352
Greenock	518	969	2,049	5,601
Ballantrae	28,335	31,897	35,064	87,154
Other Districts ...	316	456	19,299	46,669
Total	259,159	247,828	894,472	2,097,963

In the Fishing Districts of Montrose, Banff, Findhorn, Helmsdale and Wick, inshore fishing by means of the Danish seine-net has largely replaced drift-net fishing for herring since 1921. Lossiemouth was the first port to adopt this new gear. It still retains its pre-eminence as the chief seine-net port in Scotland. Arbroath, Macduff, Whitehills, Helmsdale, and many other East Coast ports followed the example of Lossiemouth.

The Danish seine-net, or *"Snurrevaed,"* usually has a span of about 160 feet and a bag of about 50-60 feet in depth. It is made of light twine, mounted on light rope. When fishing, the vessel puts out a dan or buoy to which the end of the manila rope is attached. She then pays out about 1,000 fathoms of the warp. Turning almost at right angles, she pays out the net. Moving in a semi-circle towards the starting point, the second warp is paid out. When the vessel has arrived back at the starting point, the first warp is coiled on board. Hauling on both warps, the net itself is dragged towards the vessel as the space between them is gradually narrowed. The whole operation does not usually take more than an hour, and can be repeated again and again until enough fish has been caught. The fish is gutted and boxed before the vessel arrives back in port, so that it can be landed at once. Various types of special winches and coilers are used by seine-net boats.*

More recently there have been great developments in seine-netting at Peterhead, Fraserburgh and Wick. This method of fishing has also been taken up in the Ballantrae, Campbeltown, Fort William, Shetland, Loch Broom Districts. In some places it is carried on throughout the winter as well as in summer. The newer type of dual-purpose boats engage in herring fishing in the summer and autumn, and revert to seine-netting for the rest of the year.

This method of capture ensures a regular, though limited supply of really fresh fish, for most of it is landed within a few hours of being caught. The fish can be on sale within twenty-four hours of swimming in the sea. Only a small proportion is allocated for home consumption. Most of the seine-net landings are dispatched by rail or road to markets in the south—even to London. Until quite recently it could be said that seine-net fish was only iced after it had been landed, but some of the larger vessels are now staying

*The high cost of this method of fishing in these days—as all others—will be realised from the present approximate prices: a large vessel requires 10 coils of rope at £10 each. A seine-net now costs from £30 to £50, according to size. The engine itself cost about £4000, about half the total cost of a dual-purpose boat.

away from port for a week or longer and keep their fish in ice—just the same as deep-sea trawlers.*

(b) *North and West Coasts.*

There are extensive fishing grounds all round the North and West Coasts of Scotland, but from the economic point of view the fisheries have never been of the same importance as those on the East Coast. The men have always been handicapped in the pursuit of their calling. They have often been accused of a lack of initiative, but they have never been given the right sort of encouragement, though countless schemes have been put forward to help the fishermen-crofters of the Highlands and Islands.

The situation to-day is not very different to what it was a century ago. The fishermen-crofter cannot compete with the mass production of big trawling centres such as Aberdeen, or even with the inshore fishermen on the East Coast,

---

*Quantity and Average Price per Cwt. of Chief Species of White Fish Landed.

	1938			1948		
	1000 cwts.	Average price		1000 cwts.	Average price	
		s.	d.		s.	d.
Total Fish	2,504	21	11	3,357	49	10
Haddocks	1,025	20	2	1,157	49	7
Cod and codling ...	548	18	6	671	37	9
Whitings	321	17	0	667	42	3
Lemon Soles	68	71	7	50	109	8
Plaice	70	49	8	85	100	11
Halibut	33	72	5	67	162	9
Skates and rays	84	16	10	115	41	0
Hake	34	34	8	77	91	3
Witches	20	36	10	25	62	5
Turbot	11	62	6	19	169	2
Ling	57	11	10	126	30	9
Monks	72	7	7	40	20	4
Megrims	15	31	6	16	65	0
Saithe	66	5	7	92	21	3
Torsk	32	9	8	52	32	2

Total landings by vessels with seine nets (1000 cwts.)

	Steam	Motor
1938	0.4	258.8
1948	2.5	891.9

with their fleets of up-to-date boats. Many of these work on grounds off the West Coast for part of the year. To the natives of the islands they are "poachers" just as were the English and Dutch fishermen of the seventeenth and eighteenth centuries.

The majority of the West Highland fishermen cannot afford to buy new and up-to-date boats and expensive gear. They are afraid to avail themselves of facilities now offered them under the Inshore Fisheries Act. There are still many of the fishermen-crofters who use hand-lines. On the East Coast there are hardly any women alive who know how to bait handlines, and the younger generation would not care to undertake this laborious occupation.

The *Report of the Scottish Economic Committee* published shortly before the second world war, stressed that the value of inshore fishing as an adjunct of crofting communities could not be overlooked. At the same time it made clear that, owing to the poor conditions of boats and gear, together with the lack of any satisfactory encouragement on the part of the Government,

> "older fishermen are unable to prosecute fishing profitably, and younger men are disinclined to take up the occupation. Consequently local enterprise is discouraged and the inshore fishing is in a decadent condition. The possibility is that unless the local men are encouraged to take up fishing efficiently and in earnest, their fishing grounds will be more and more exploited by fishermen from the East Coast of Scotland (or from England), many of whom, owing to the depression in the herring fishing industry, are finding it necessary to resort more extensively to white fishing."

The Inshore Fishing Industry Act, 1945, made grants up to a total of £500,000 and loans up to a total of £800,000 to inshore fishermen for the acquisition, improvement and reconditioning of boats and the purchase of gear. The White Fish and Herring Industries Act of 1948 increased the amount available to inshore fishermen by the 1945 Act to £1,000,000 in grants and £1,800,000 in loans. At the close of 1948, 813 Scottish inshore fishermen had been helped to acquire or recondition 342 motor-boats; 134 of which were new vessels The 1948 Act also provides to loan to any co-operative scheme for assisting inshore fishermen, to meet capital expenditure in their business. So far only a few attempts to fish with seine nets have been made by native fishermen in the Hebrides, and most of them consider that it will pay better to develop the lobster fisheries.

(c) *Shell Fisheries.*

Lobsters are the most profitable species of shell-fish landed in Scotland as will be seen from the following table—

	Lobsters				Crabs			
938	803,414	£52,691	1s	4d	1,260,861	£9,033	1s	7d
948	1,465,060	£271,453	3s	8d	3,118,734	£105,164	8s	1d

Lobsters are caught almost everywhere round our coasts, but the chief centres are the Orkneys, Outer Hebrides, certain parts of the Fishing Districts of Loch Broom, Loch Carron and Fort William, and the southern half of the East Coast from Fife to the Border. Crabs—called "partans" on the Moray Firth coast—are taken in larger quantities from the North Sea. They are highly a perishable form of shell-fish, and not suitable for the uncertain and slow modes of transport from the Outer Hebrides to the Mainland.

As was pointed out in the *Report on the Highlands and Islands* issued by the Scottish Economic Committee in 1938, lobster fishing is peculiarly suitable to the crofter-fisherman, as it can be associated with work on the croft, and as the demand for lobster is steady from year to year, though there are seasonal fluctuations, the fishing, if properly conducted, is capable of yielding a good return for a moderate outlay. Assistance is now being given by the *Scottish Agricultural Organisation Society* for boats suitable for lobster fishing, but so far not very much has been done in this respect. The same body is now operating lobster ponds at Bernera (Lewis) and Stockinish (Harris). The former pond was constructed about eighty years ago. More ponds, or alternative methods of storage, are urgently needed in the Outer Hebrides and elsewhere. Meanwhile experience is being gained in packing and marketing, There have been experiments in the freezing and cooking of lobsters before marketing. Perhaps one of the chief difficulties in promoting any of these schemes is that the Hebridean fishermen—unlike those of the East Coast—are not yet accustomed to borrowing large sums of money.

The greatest amount of crabs are landed in the Eyemouth and Fraserburgh Fishery Districts, also in the Anstruther, Leith and Wick Districts. Elsewhere crabs are of not much commercial importance. Clams are mostly caught on the Firth of Clyde. Mussels are chiefly gathered in the Montrose district. At one time the oyster beds in Loch Ryan, Wigtownshire, were very productive.*

Perhaps more could be done regarding the other types of shell fish, such as cockles and whelks, which are not made use of in Scotland as they are in England. The oyster industry certainly needs reviving in Scotland.

(d) *Salmon Fisheries.*

Salmon fishing with nets, laid within a short distance from the land, is carried on in many parts of the East and West Coasts of Scotland. In 1939 about 2,000 men were engaged in the commercial salmon net fishing. The number to-day is probably less than this. Salmon nets can only be worked by the owners or by persons holding licenses from them. The men employed are not independent fishermen, but wage-earners. The fishing season lasts from March to August. The value of salmon landed varies considerably from year to year. Most of the fish is sent to inland markets in England and Scotland. Direct statistics of the catches of salmon landed are not obtainable. Railway and steamship returns show the weight of salmon transported in Scotland during the years 1938 and 1948.

1938	1,229 tons
1948	935 tons

The average value of the catch in these same years was—

1938	£286,766
1948	£575,960

The once extensive and profitable export trade of dried or cured salmon came to an end early in the last century, mainly as a result of the sudden development of the herring industry.

*Year	Mussels	Oysters
1938	£4,142	£622
1948	£3,018	£354

Salmon fishermen form a class of their own, and have little or no association with others. During the summer months they are hard at work, taking salmon from the nets, for which purpose motor-cobles are used. Throughout the year there is always much to be done ashore, mending nets and looking after other gear required. Each salmon fishing station usually employs about a dozen men during the season.

CHAPTER VIII.

FISHING VESSELS—OLD AND NEW.

Until well on in the present century, Scotland retained several types of fishing vessels that were quite different to those found in England. Even to-day, when standardisation in all forms of life has become the rule, fishing craft are being built in our ports which still have a definite local character.

In the Orkneys and Shetland, which did not become part of Scotland until the middle of the fifteenth century, we find the oldest types of boats. The smaller Shetland open fishing boats are almost identical with those in Norway. Until about the middle of the last century, the wood for these boats was usually brought over from Norway, owing to the lack of timber in the islands. In these cases the woodwork was already cut to shape, and the parts had only to be assembled on arrival. The Shetland boats were "*sixerns*" (six-oared) and "*fourareens*" (four-oared). A few lairds had "great boats"—either "*auchtoarings*" or "*twaloarings.*" Their lines had undergone little change since the Norsemen first settled in the islands about 620. If a dragon's head were added to the stem and a tail to the stern, a nineteenth century sixern or fourareen could pass for a miniature "long-ship" akin to the Gokstad and Oseberg types.

The sixerns (Old Norse "*sexaeringr*") were clinker-built vessels of fir and fastened with iron. The method of construction was similar to that of the Viking ships. The widely spaced ribs were connected with the keel by garboard strakes. Their average overall length was about 28 feet; 16 to 18 feet keel; 8 to 10 feet beam, and 3 feet depth in hold. The rig consisted of a single square sail. The mast was stepped about amidships. The tack was made fast to the fore-quarter, not to the stem head. The sail had one or two reefs in the head, and two or three in the foot. Instead of a traveller, a cow's horn or a piece of hard wood was used. It was called the "rakki" and was secured to the yard by seizings.

All Shetland oars are square in the loom and cannot be feathered. Pieces of hard wood are nailed on the loom on

"ZULU."

the part that slides on the rowth, and on the part that presses against the *"kabe,"* i.e. the flat wooden thole-pin fitted into the rowth, *"humble-baands"*—grommets of cow's hide, whale sinew or rope, pass through a hole in the rowth, round the loom of the oar and the "kabe," giving sufficient play

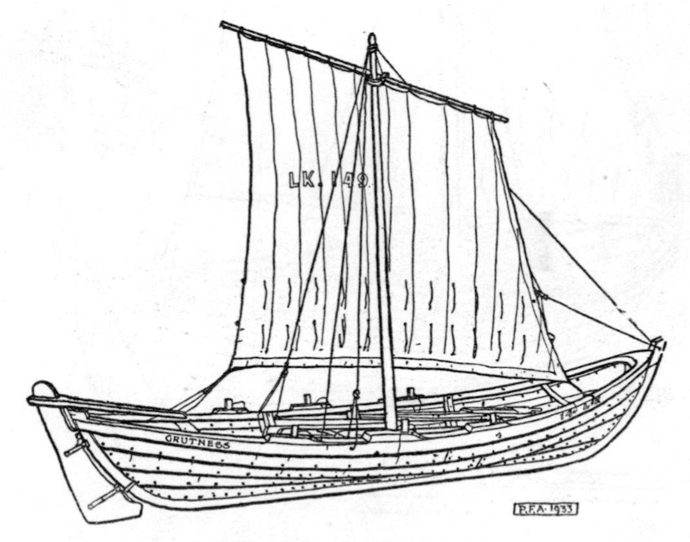

SHETLAND "FOURAREEN."

to enable the oar to slide aft, preparatory to a fresh stroke being taken when pulling.

Sixerns were divided into six "rooms" (old Norse *'rúm*) or compartments—the forehead, foreroom, midroom, austroom or waderoom, shot, and "kannie" or "hurrik." Each "room" was separated from the other by *"fiska-brods"* (fish-boards). Every other part of the boat had its own special Norse name*

Sixerns are now obsolete, but fourareens are still found everywhere in Shetland.

---

*See article in *The Mariner's Mirror* (August, 1921) by R. Stuart Bruce; also J. Spence's *Shetland Folk-Lore*, p. 32, etc.

The *Fair Isle skiff* is another type of Shetland boat, much smaller than the sixern. It carries a square-sail and three pairs of ten foot oars. A Fair Isle skiff is even more Norse in her lines than a sixern or fourareen. The midship section is very flat, the bow and stern pointed. Average

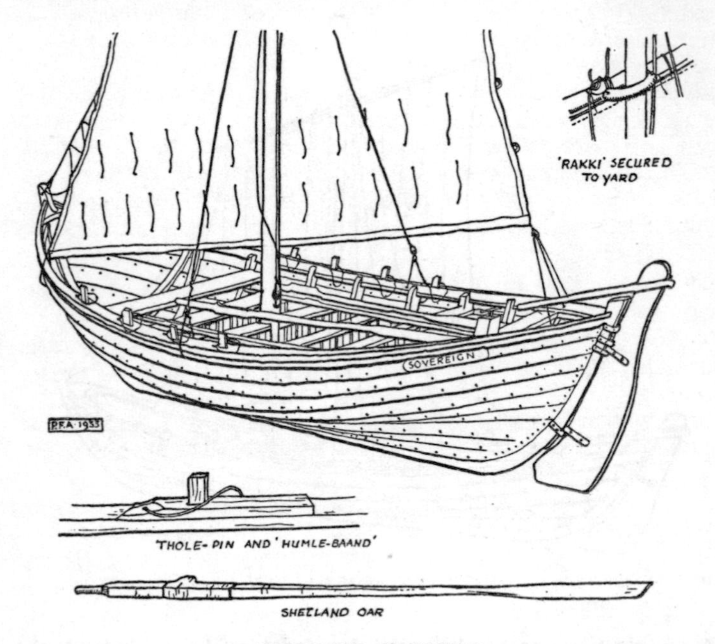

SHETLAND "SIXERN."

dimensions are: Length over-all, 20-22 feet; length on keel, 15 feet; breadth, 5.7 feet, depth amidships, 1.6 feet; depth aft, about 3 feet.

The *Ness yole*, used for inshore fishing, was very lightly built, with only five pairs of ribs—not bolted to the keel, but connected with it by the garboard strake. A square sail was used. Average dimensions were: Length over all, 23 feet; length of keel, 15 feet; breadth, 5.5 feet; depth, 1.5 feet.

In the Orkneys the favourite types of boat were the *North Isles* or *Westray yole*, and the *South Isles boat*.

These were double-ended, clinker-built vessels of Norwegian pine planking on oak frames. These yoles had a much greater beam and fuller stern than the typical Shetland sixern or fourareen. It has been pointed out that she showed the intermediate stage in the evolution of the "skaffie" clinker-built boat with curved stem and raking stern, almost universal on the Moray Firth until about 1880. The rig consisted of two standing lug-sails and a jib. The mainsail was extended by means of a traveller which worked on a long boom fitted with a goose-neck. The two pairs of oars were worked between double thole-pins, which replaced the single kabe and grummet of the Shetland boats. Average dimensions were: Length over all, 19 feet; length on keel, 14 feet; breadth, 9.9 feet; depth amidships, 2.8 feet; depth aft, 3.5 feet.

The South Isles yole was similar in construction to the boats used in the North Isles, but carried two sprit-sails.

For the cod fisheries about the middle of the last century, the Shetlanders used *deep-sea smacks,* from 20 to 90 tons register. They carried from twelve to sixteen hands. There was not much to distinguish them from the Grimsby smacks, in fact many of them were bought second-hand from England. About 1876 the native Shetland craft were gradually replaced by "Fifies," and other types of vessels purchased second-hand from Moray Firth and other Scottish ports. Most of them were given a cutter or dandy rig in place of the original lug-sails.

It is difficult to trace back the history of fishing boats on mainland of Scotland previous to the middle of the last century. In 1849 a Report was presented to the House of Commons which gave details of six types of Scottish fishing vessels. In 1883 Captain Swinburne published a pamphlet containing five diagrams of boats commonly used at that date. Each has her own characteristic features.

The *"Skaffie"* was an obvious development from the boats of Norse origin. She was larger and latterly completely decked. The rake of the stern post and her curved stem were unusual. About 1855 Skaffies were used on the south coast of the Moray Firth as far east as Portsoy. From about 1880 they were gradually replaced by Zulu boats. Skaffies sometimes carried a mizen in addition to the fore and main lug-sails, with poles or spars rigged up to act as bow-lines. The early Skaffies were three-masted open boats. The midship section was low and broad; the "floor" flat and rather hollow. The dimensions varied considerably from 40 to 45 feet over all; 25 to 36 feet length of keel; breadth,

"SKAFFIE."

13 to 17 feet; depth in hold, 7 to 9 feet. These *"scaiths"*—as they were sometimes called—sailed fast, and stood up well to the wind. Five men were the normal crew.

The Aberdeen, Peterhead, Fraserburgh and Wick boats of the middle of the last century had rounded sterns, and stems, with only slight rakes. The raked stern was peculiar to the Skaffie.

The most common type of Scottish fishing vessel until about the introduction of steam was the *"Fifie."* They were to be found right up the East Coast from Berwickshire to midway along the coast of Banffshire, also on the north side of the Moray Firth; Aberdeen, Peterhead, Fraserburgh and later on in the Orkneys and Shetland. Until 1855 they were undecked and of small size. Their characteristic features were vertical and comparatively sharp bows and sterns.

The rig consisted of a high dipping lug-sail forward, and a small standing lug-sail aft. Originally they were clinker-built, but later on carvel built Fifies became the rule. A century ago the average Fifie measured only from 30 to 25 feet of keel. But later on they grew larger and larger until many of them were 75 feet long, and from 25 tons register. Out-rigged spars, known as "booms," were used with the sails in fine weather. The dimensions of the Fifie were:

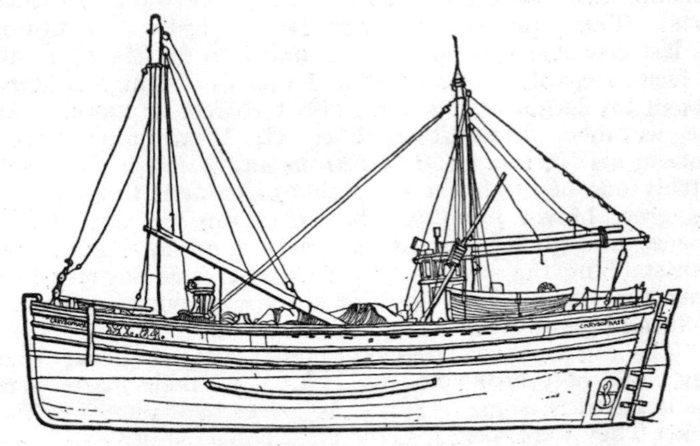

"FIFIE" (MASTS CUT-DOWN AND MOTOR INSTALLED).

length over all, 50 to 75 feet, length of keel, 44 to 68 feet; breadth, about 17.5 feet, depth in hold from 7 to 8 feet.

A smaller type of Fifie was the Leith "*Baldie,*" used mainly for inshore fishing. She was a low-built, open yawl of from 15 to 24 feet, with breadth of about 5 to 8 feet, and depth of 3 feet 6 inches. Most of them were carvel-built. On the Moray Firth coast they were known as "*skiffs.*" They were light enough to use two pairs of 12 feet oars, but they depended mostly on a tall dipping lug-sail, hoisted on a lofty raked mast, stepped far forward. A few of the larger Baldies carried a jib and a standing lug-sail. The name Baldie (pronounced "Bauldie") is said to be a contraction for "Garibaldi."

In 1878, William Campbell of Lossiemouth decided to combine the good points of the "Fifie" and "Skaffie" models, and had a boat built, the *Nonsuch,* which had the raked stern of the latter and the sharp stem of the former. The story is told that he wanted one type of boat, his wife the other. So they went fifty-fifty.* Somebody nicknamed the novel type of vessel "*Zulu,*" a war in South Africa having just been concluded. The name stuck, and to this day, all Scottish fishing boats with long raked sterns are commonly known as "Zulus." At first they were only to be found on the south side of the Moray Firth coast from Macduff westwards, but later on they were built for other ports. They grew larger and larger during the 'nineties of the last century, some of them running to 61 feet keel and 86 feet over all. The combined rakes of stem and stern post in the largest Zulus were about 20 feet or more. As late as 1906, Lieut-Commander H. Warington Smyth wrote in his *Mast and Sail in Europe and Asia* (p. 112): "it is truly one of the finest sea sights of modern times to see this great brown pyramid come marching up out of the horizon, and go leaning by you at a ten-knot speed, the peak stabbing the sky as it lurches past some seventy feet above the water. The sense of strain and power is not so produced by any work of man at sea."

The big Zulus carried enormous sails, so heavy that they could only be hoisted by steam, and their masts were like large trees, some as much as 2 feet in diameter at the deck.† They were, perhaps, the most noble fishing craft ever designed in Britain.

---

*A more probable explanation of the origin of the Zulu fishing vessel is that about 1880, fishermen began to go to more distant waters for herring, consequently there was a great need for a more powerful boat. Mr James Smith (Buckie) points out that "from the builder's point of view, a straight stem was more easily obtained in one piece for the bigger craft than the curved stem of the Skaffie. The straight stem with a slight rake forward meant a longer keel too. The result was the Zulu type which amply proved herself to be a more able boat than the Skaffie, and was quicker in stays than the Fifie. The large Fifie boat, however, was steadier 'running' because of her very long keel and bottom. The long under-rake of the Zulu stern protected her rudder when worked in port." Moreover a Zulu stern was more simple to build than that of a Fifie, so, altogether this famous type of boat may have been nothing more than the logical result of economy and functional requirements.

†Zulu oars (Sweeps) were square at the loom with hard-wood clamps to take the wear of the double thole-pins. These great oars were "feathered" by the makers and each boat had port and starboard oars, known on the Moray Firth as "efferaw" and "fawar" oars.

Between 1870 and 1890 a small number of *smack-rigged* herring-boats were built on parts of the East Coast.* It was maintained that this rig was handier to work in the lochs and sounds of the West Highlands and Shetland. There was always a risk of accidents with great lug sails of the Fifies and Zulus.

In the Hebrides a popular type of boat about the middle of the last century was the *Stornoway yawl*, which was used for long-line fishing until replaced latterly by Fifies and Zulus, bought from the East Coast. The average boat was

LOCH FYNE BOATS.

from 20 to 25 feet in keel, and 25 to 30 feet over all; broad in beam, and with raked stern and stem. Broad, low lugsails were carried. The crew consisted of five or six men. When working the line, oars were often used.

For the herring and great-line fishing on Loch Fyne and the Firth of Clyde the most common type of boat used

---

*Early in the present century a number of what were called "Islay boats," of 20 to 25 keel were built at Buckie for the West Coast.

in the last century was the "*Nabby.*" This craft had a small fore-deck, which provided shelter for a crew of three or four men, and was clinker or carvel built. The average dimensions were: Length over all 32 to 34 feet; length of keel 24 to 28 feet; depth aft, 3½ to 6 feet; depth forward 1 to 2 feet. The rig consisted of a lug and jib. A mizen was sometimes carried in fine weather. These boats were also used for ring-net fishing for herring and worked in pairs.

There were many local variations in the Firth of Clyde boats, for instance the *Dunure* and *Maidens skiffs* were usually square-sterned, and narrower, than those used on the upper waters of the Firth and on Loch Fyne. On the Ayrshire coast, small, long, low narrow skiffs, carrying a lug and jib were used for line fishing. Ballantrae, owing to the lack of a harbour, had to be content with a 22 feet skiff for all kinds of fishing. The *Portpatrick line boat* resembled the Orkney yole. She was very beamy, with a full bow and and quarters. She carried two lug-sails. Average dimensions were: Keel, 16 feet; beam, 7 feet; depth inside, 2½ feet.

Some of the *Stranraer yawls* during the latter half of the last century looked like miniature "Zulus" above the water-line. The mast was as much raked as the stern.

Sixty years ago Manx-built *luggers* could be found in some parts of the West Coast, and a number of *Manx "Dandies"* and *ketches* were bought for Shetland owners. They were used for the mackerel and herring fishing off Ireland in the spring, and for the herring fishing on the East Coast in summer.

Annan, on the Solway Firth, had its own type of boat, used for trawling. The original boats were built on More cambe Bay between 1860 and 1870. They had square sterns and were clinker-built. Later on carvel-built boats became common. All were decked, but had a small open hatchway. Their lines resembled those of a yacht. The rig was always a mainsail, gaff-topsail, foresail and jib—similar to the rig of almost every fishing boat of the North West coasts of England. After 1900 a faster and lighter model was introduced, with a short curved stem, and very raked keel and stern-post. Average dimensions were: Length over all, 36 to 39 feet; length on water-line, 30 to 34 feet; breadth, 9.8 feet to 11 feet, draught of water, 4 feet. When trawling for flounders in water, two men made up the crew.

During the summer shrimping, one man often worked alone, or had a boy with him.

The *first steam fishing boat* built in Scotland was launched at Aberdeen in 1871. Most of these early steam fishing vessels were ketch-rigged, and only used their engines as an auxiliary to sails. Except for a tall funnel, they did not differ much from a ketch-rigged Fifie. The early steam trawlers were queer looking vessels, with wheel-houses aft of the funnels. All the steam drifters built within 1900 and 1920 had much the same lines. At first they were built of wood and then of iron, but later on many steel vessels were laid down.

The average *Scottish drifter,* many of which are still fishing, although over forty years old, has the following approximate dimensions: Length, 80 to 90 feet; beam about 18 feet; depth of hold, 8 feet 8 inches; draught about 10 feet; gross tonnage, 80 to 85; engine, 28 to 33 h.p.

When new, a speed of from 10 knots was possible. There are two masts. A small sail is sometimes set from the mizen. With a fair wind a balloon-jib used to be set on the foremast; the sheet coming well aft of the mast. The foremast is lowered when the drifter is fishing. Characteristic features of the typical Scottish steam drifter are a single flush deck and a bold sheer; a straight stem and a deep counter stern. Some recent drifters have cruiser sterns. The 9 feet square fish-hold takes up the greater part of the forward deck space. The superstructure is smaller than that of a trawler. Scottish drifters are more graceful and less dumpy than those found in most English ports. It is easy to distinguish them. At one time almost every Scottish port had its own methods of painting, and colour schemes. At Buckie, for instance, most drifters had badges or coats of arms on their funnels.

It is worth mentioning that the first application of power to fishing purposes took place when steam capstans were fitted to sailing vessels, about 1880. The steam was also used for setting sail and for barking nets. The first steam drifters were often called "pipe stalkies" because of their thin, tall funnels.

The *steam trawlers* working from Scottish ports are similar to those found in England, except that most of them are smaller and far older. Only at Aberdeen do we find a few up-to-date vessels such as those registered at Hull and Grimsby.

It was in 1907 that the first fishing vessel in Scotland was fitted with a paraffin engine. Twenty years later the *Marigold* of Lossiemouth was the first boat to be given a Diesel engine. After the first World-War, motor fishing vessels gradually replaced sailing craft for all white fishing, especially when the Danish seine-net began to supersede lines from 1921 onwards. The typical *Scottish seine-net craft* has a flush deck with a bold sheer, a small wheel house aft (in the larger vessels the galley is often combined with the wheelhouse), and two masts. The dimensions are: Length over all, 50 to 75 feet; beam, 15 feet 10 inches to 19 feet 3 inches; draught, 5 feet 3 inches to 9 feet; speed, 7½ to 9½ knots; bunkers 300 to 1,000 gallons. Various types of engines are fitted—66-160-250 h.p.

During the second World-War, the Admiralty built what were known as "M.F.Vs." for various duties, intend-

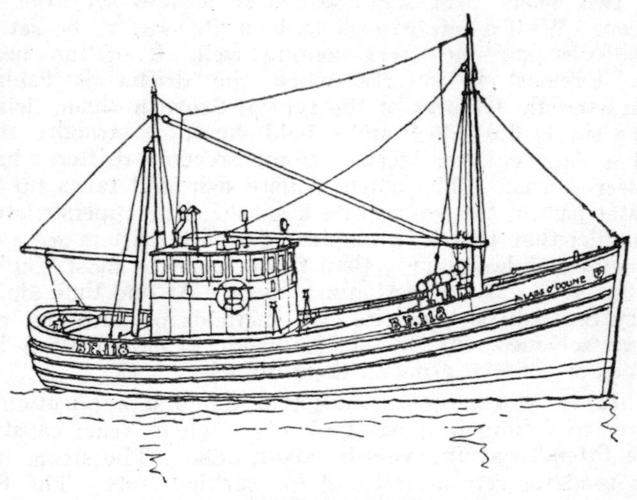

"LASS O' DOUNE" (MACDUFF, 1949).

ing that they should be used for fishing on the cessation of hostilities. They have wooden hulls and Diesel engines. Many of these vessels, whose length varies from 45 to 61½,

75 and 90 feet, have now been reconditioned and are being used by Scottish fishermen as drifters and seine-netters.

The Herring Industry Board has recently built two experimental dual-purpose motor driven craft, with a view to perfecting an economical and efficient type of fishing vessel suitable for present day conditions.

In most modern motor fishing vessels of the larger type, the cabin is placed aft, because a compression ignition engine gives off little heat. A "cruiser-stern" is now almost universal.* A combination deck-house-galley and wheel-house is becoming more and more popular. In smaller boats the crew usually have their quarters forward, the engine being placed right aft. All larger craft are now fitted with echometers, wireless direction finders, and have radio telephony installed. The accommodation for the crew is luxurious when compared with that in older vessels. even steam-drifters. There are important boat-building yards at St Monans, Aberdeen, Peterhead, Fraserburgh, Sandhaven, Macduff, Banff, Buckie, Lossiemouth and Lerwick.

As a general rule the fishermen of the Firth of Clyde and some of the Firth of Forth ports seem to fancy varnished hulls, whereas elsewhere painted hulls—either black or red—are al most universal. Aberdeen trawlers are usually painted green, with red between the waterline and deck line.

---

*The first fishing vessel with a cruiser-stern was the "Ovoca"; built by J. Tyrrell and Sons at Arklow, Co. Wexford, in 1907.

MAPS

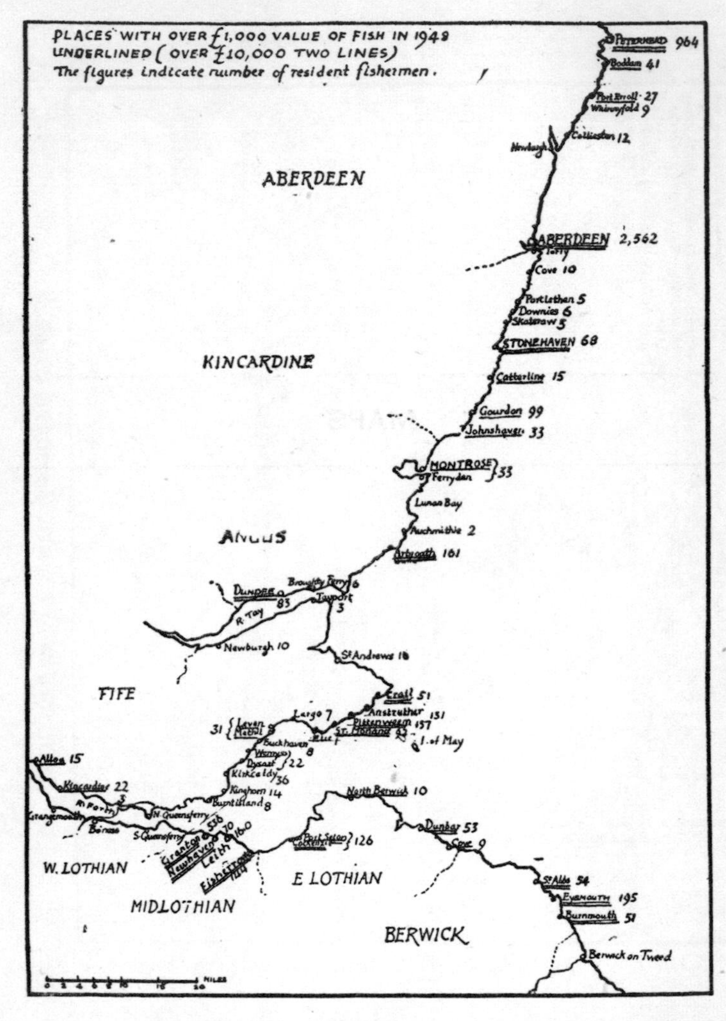
PLACES WITH OVER £1,000 VALUE OF FISH IN 1948
UNDERLINED (OVER £10,000 TWO LINES)
The figures indicate number of resident fishermen.
PETERHEAD 964
Boddam 41
Port Erroll 27
Whinnyfold 9
Collieston 12
ABERDEEN
ABERDEEN 2,562
Torry
Cove 10
Portlethen 5
Downies 6
Skateraw 5
STONEHAVEN 68
KINCARDINE
Catterline 15
Gourdon 99
Johnshaven 33
MONTROSE
Ferryden
33
Lunan Bay
Auchmithie 2
ANGUS
Arbroath 161
Broughty Ferry 6
Dundee 83
Tayport 3
R. Tay
Newburgh 10
St Andrews 16
FIFE
Crail 51
Anstruther 131
Largo 7
Pittenweem 157
St. Monance
31 { Leven Methil
I. of May
Buckhaven 8
Dysart 22
Kirkcaldy 36
Alloa 15
Kinghorn 14
Burntisland 8
R. Forth
Grangemouth
N. Queensferry
S. Queensferry
Granton 536
Newhaven 70
Leith 160
North Berwick 10
Dunbar 53
Cove 9
Port Seton 126
W. LOTHIAN
E LOTHIAN
MIDLOTHIAN
St Abbs 54
Eyemouth 195
Burnmouth 51
BERWICK
Berwick on Tweed
0 2 4 6 8 10 15 20 MILES

(I) BERWICK-ON-TWEED TO PETERHEAD.

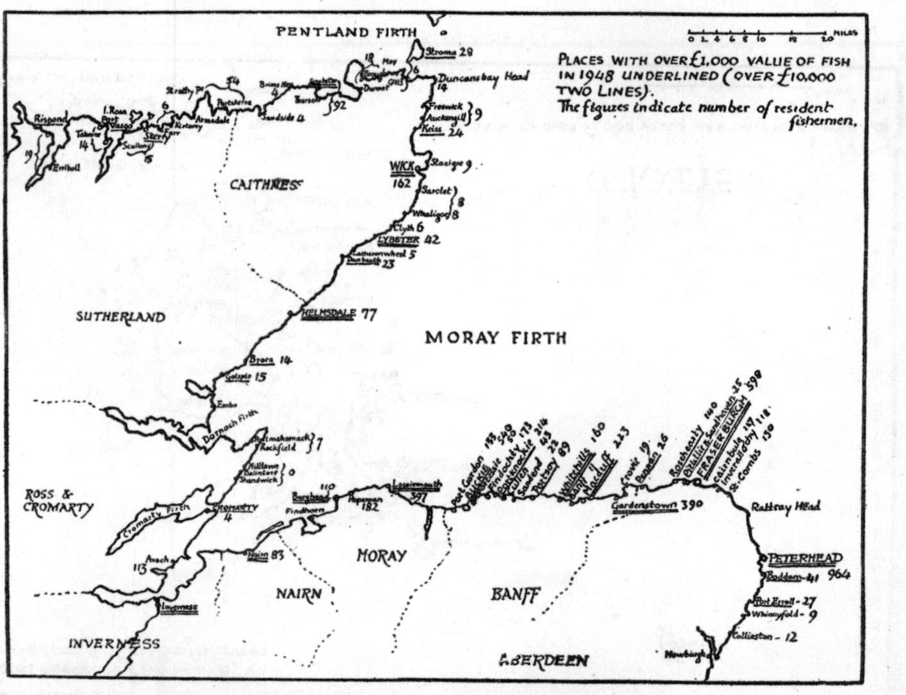

(II) THE MORAY FIRTH and NORTH COAST.

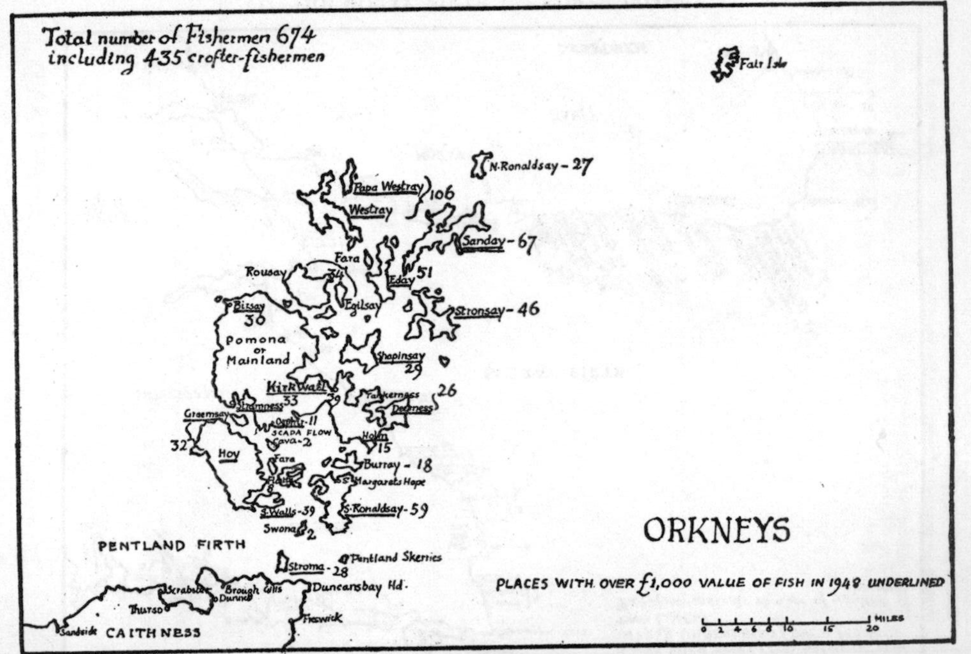

(III) THE ORKNEYS.

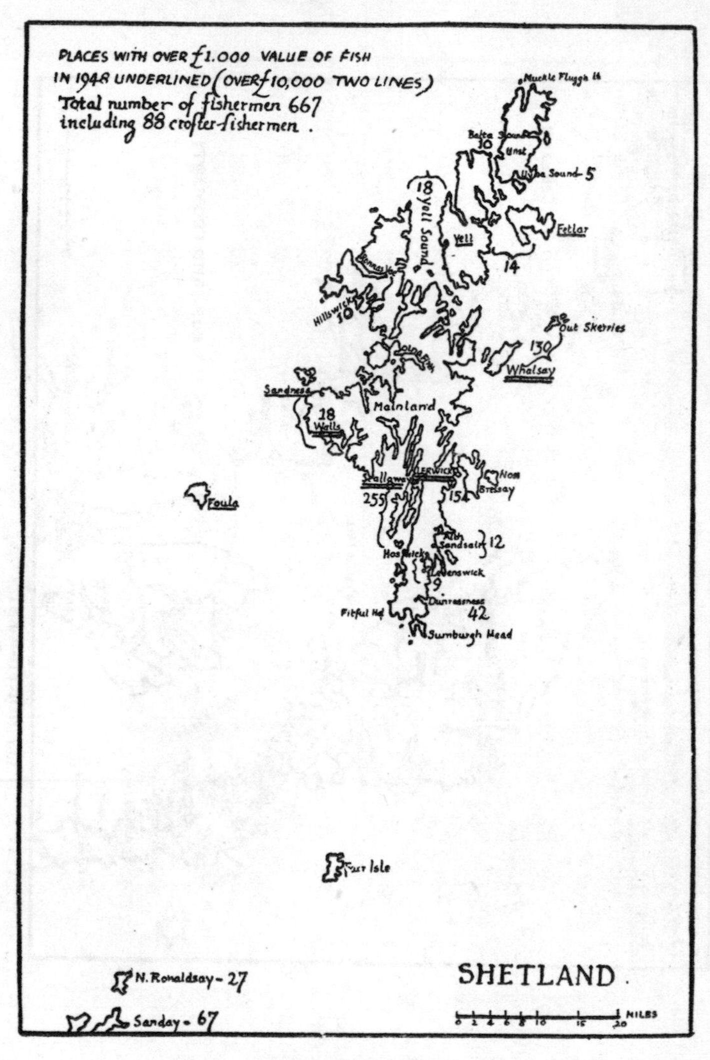
PLACES WITH OVER £1.000 VALUE OF FISH
IN 1948 UNDERLINED (OVER £10,000 TWO LINES)
Total number of fishermen 667
including 88 crofter-fishermen.
Muckle Flugga
Balta Sound
10
Unst
Sound - 5
18
Yell Sound
Yell
Fetlar
14
Hillswick
10
Out Skerries
130
Whalsay
Sandness
Mainland
18
Walls
Lerwick
Noss
Bressay
255
154
Foula
Sandsair
12
Leven swick
9
Dunrossness
42
Fitful Hd
Sumburgh Head
Isle
N. Ronaldsay - 27
Sanday - 67
SHETLAND.
0 2 4 6 8 10 15 20 MILES

(IV) SHETLAND.

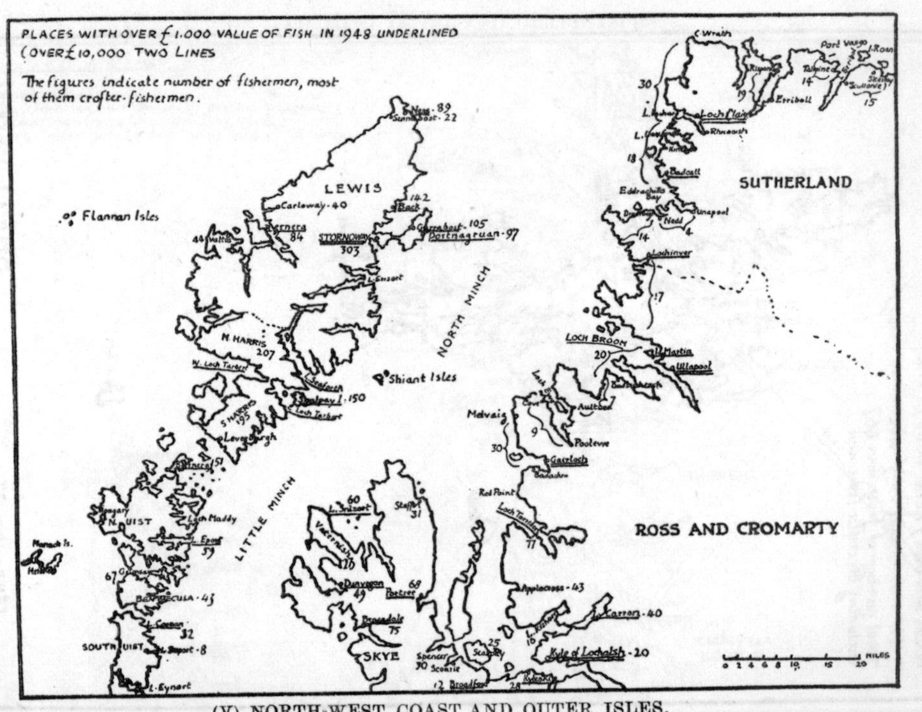

(V) NORTH-WEST COAST AND OUTER ISLES.

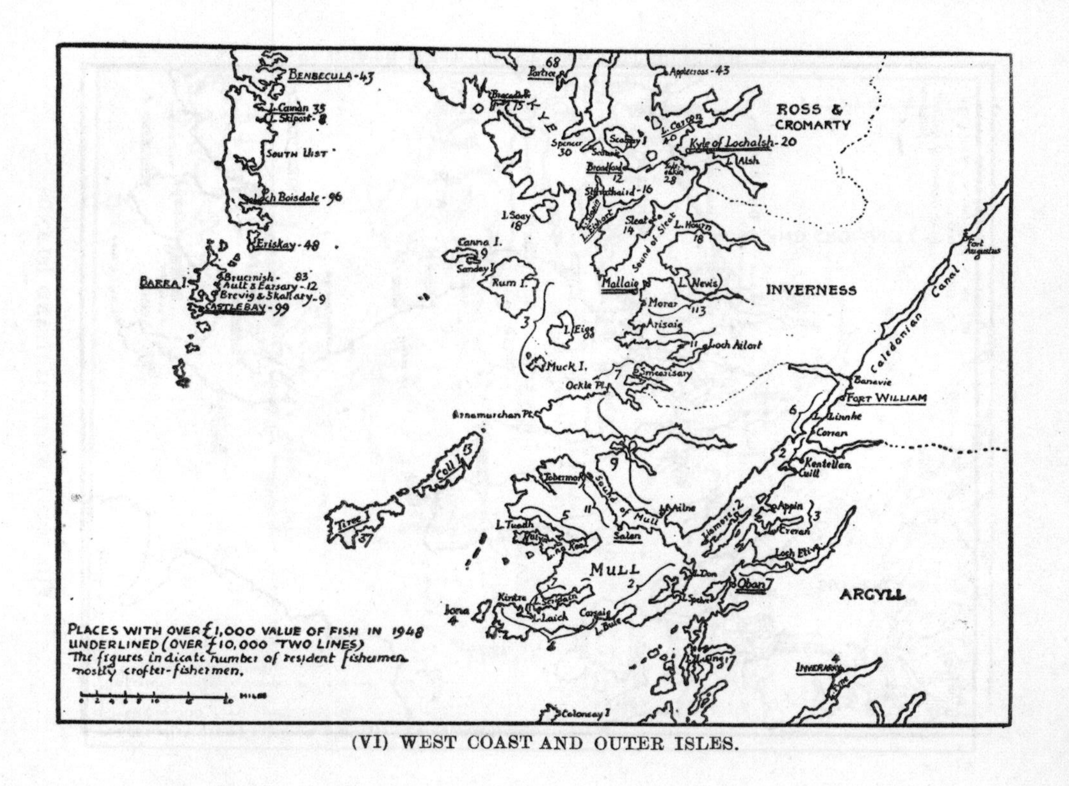

(VI) WEST COAST AND OUTER ISLES.

(VII) SOUTH-WEST COAST AND ISLANDS.

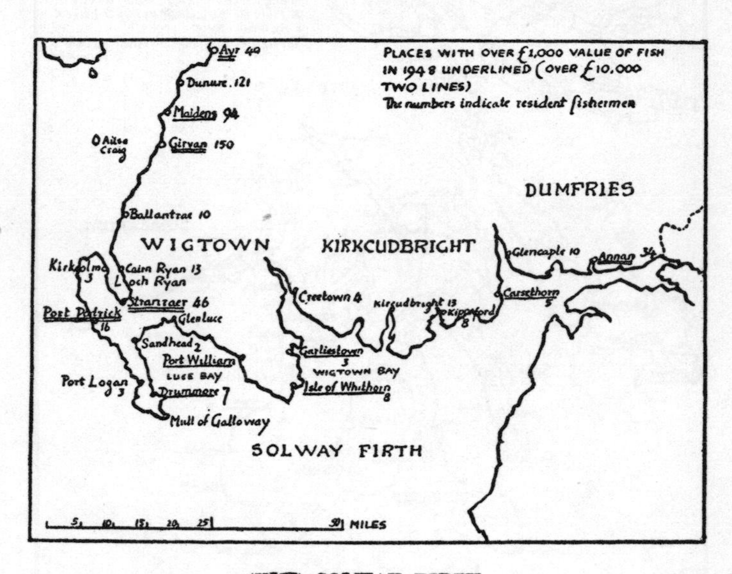
PLACES WITH OVER £1,000 VALUE OF FISH IN 1948 UNDERLINED (OVER £10,000 TWO LINES)
The numbers indicate resident fishermen
Ayr 40
Dunure. 121
Maidens 94
Girvan 150
Ailsa Craig
Ballantrae 10
WIGTOWN
KIRKCUDBRIGHT
DUMFRIES
Kirkcolm 3
Cairn Ryan 13
Loch Ryan
Stranraer 46
Port Patrick 16
Glenluce
Sandhead 2
Port William
LUCE BAY
Port Logan 3
Drummore 7
Mull of Galloway
Creetown 4
Kircudbright 13
Kippford 8
Garlieston 3
WIGTOWN BAY
Isle of Whithorn 8
Glencaple 10
Annan 34
Carsethorn 5
SOLWAY FIRTH
5 10 15 20 25 50 MILES

(VIII) SOLWAY FIRTH.

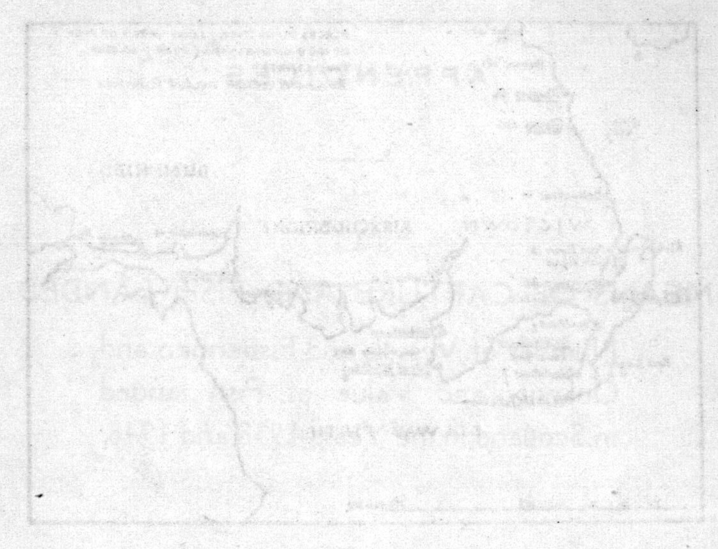

APPENDICES

---

(1)

MEANS OF CAPTURE AND FISH LANDED

Number of Vessels and Fishermen and Quantity and Value of Fish landed in Scotland in the Years 1938 and 1948.

Place.	Fishing Craft. 30 feet keel and upwards.*			Under 30 feet keel.		Total.		Fishermen.	Quantity and Value of Fish Landed by British Vessels. Herrings.		Other kinds (except Shell Fish).		Value of Shell Fish.
	Steam	Motor	Sail	Motor	Sail	No.	Tons	No.	Cwts.	£	Cwts.	£	£
Eyemouth District.													
Burnmouth	—	9	—	5	7	21	104	64	—	—	746	378	3,278
Eyemouth	12	17	—	4	—	33	866	232	42,932	17,080	11,963	13,588	4
St Abbs	—	4	—	13	1	18	132	70	—	—	713	278	1,536
Totals	12	30	—	22	8	72	1,102	366	42,932	17,080	13,422	14,244	4,818
Leith District.													
Cove	—	—	—	5	—	5	16	12	—	—	310	164	1,697
Dunbar	—	1	—	13	6	20	61	38	402	113	375	318	1,687
North Berwick	—	—	—	7	—	7	18	16	6	3	20	31	475
Port Seton and Cockenzie	—	36	—	5	1	42	507	218	14	8	12,346	18,137	274
Fisherrow	—	26	—	3	—	29	445	172	—	—	50	111	78
Leith	†16	—	—	—	—	16	1,478	162					
Newhaven	—	11	—	6	1	18	200	93	173,206	66,716	406,340	396,881	946
Granton	†44	—	—	—	—	44	4,068	440					
Bo'ness													
North and South													
Queensferry	—	3	—	3	—	6	45	11	832	304	52	22	—
Grangemouth													
Alloa	—	7	2	1	9	19	108	29	—	—	888	368	—
Kincardine	—	4	1	1	—	6	62	10	—	—	1,594	240	—
Burntisland	—	—	—	—	1	1	1	2	—	—	—	—	—
Kinghorn	—	—	—	—	5	5	4	7	2	2	48	48	—
Kirkcaldy	—	—	—	14	21	35	58	46	38	20	1,593	1,332	—
Dysart and Wemyss	—	—	—	7	5	12	14	21	—	—	414	521	—
Totals	†60	88	3	65	49	265	7,085	1,277	174,500	67,166	424,030	418,173	5,157

*Drifters or Liners except as distinguished. †Trawlers.

Place.	Fishing Craft. 30 feet keel and upwards.*			Under 30 feet keel.		Total.		Fishermen.	Quantity and Value of Fish Landed by British Vessels. Herrings.		Other kinds (except Shell Fish).		Value of Shell Fish.
	Steam	Motor	Sail	Motor	Sail	No.	Tons	No.	Cwts.	£	Cwts.	£	£
Eyemouth District.													
Burnmouth	—	8	—	6	2	16	107	51	—	—	541	927	32,190
Eyemouth	1	26	—	13	—	40	875	195	3,968	4,733	45,867	76,691	7,005
St. Abbs	—	2	—	16	2	20	93	54	—	—	3,422	6,046	12,769
Totals	1	36	—	35	4	76	1,075	300	3,968	4,733	49,830	83,664	51,964
Leith District.													
Cove	—	—	—	4	2	6	13	9	—	—	—	—	2,379
Dunbar	—	3	—	21	2	26	117	53	—	—	4,591	13,179	7,901
North Berwick	—	1	—	8	—	9	47	10	—	—	93	223	3,769
Port Seton and Cockenzie	—	22	—	9	1	32	392	126	—	—	7,073	22,663	1,829
Fisherrow	—	23	—	2	—	25	454	144	12	18	50	38	—
Leith	†13	—	—	—	—	13	1,409	160	—	—	—	—	—
Newhaven	—	12	—	8	—	20	319	70	6,749	8,142	22,570	17,342	3,238
Granton	†44	—	—	—	—	44	4,576	536	9,689	12,045	642,474	1,786,506	—
Bo'ness, North and South Queensferry and Grangemouth	—	—	—	1	1	2	4	3	—	—	—	—	—
Alloa	—	6	1	3	5	15	89	15	—	—	1,168	1,247	—
Kincardine	—	8	2	—	1	11	133	22	—	—	2,781	1,259	—
Burntisland	—	—	—	5	—	5	9	8	15	19	—	—	204
Kinghorn	—	—	—	6	1	7	11	14	—	—	5	9	—
Kirkcaldy	—	—	—	14	8	22	45	36	—	—	253	685	—
Dysart and Wemyss	—	1	—	11	6	18	36	22	—	—	610	1,465	708
Totals	†57	76	3	92	27	255	7,654	1,228	16,465	20,224	681,668	1,844,616	20,028

*Drifters or Liners except as distinguished. †Trawlers.

Place.	Fishing Craft. 30 feet keel and upwards.*			Under 30 feet keel.		Total.		Fishermen.	Quantity and Value of Fish Landed by British Vessels. Herrings.		Other kinds (except Shell Fish).		Value of Shell Fish.
	Steam	Motor	Sail	Motor	Sail	No.	Tons	No.	Cwts.	£	Cwts.	£	£
Anstruther District.													
Buckhaven	—	—	—	4	2	6	17	14	—	—	34	46	2
Methil and Leven ...	—	—	—	—	2	2	3	4	3,997	1,744	180	242	3
Largo	—	—	—	3	2	5	8	14	—	—	234	190	—
Elie and Earlsferry	—	—	—	1	1	2	3	4	—	—	47	34	54
St Monance	4	33	—	4	1	42	1,216	276	35,070	11,079	2,977	4,623	—
Pittenweem	—	19	—	17	1	37	459	161	11,760	3,009	10,117	11,119	8
Anstruther and Cellardyke	19	7	—	1	6	33	992	252	97,769	30,255	389	375	836
Crail	—	—	—	12	6	18	48	39	4,599	1,229	65	48	2,878
Kingsbarns	—	—	—	—	—	—	—	1	—	—	—	—	26
St Andrews	—	—	—	6	3	9	30	18	434	97	49	61	22
River Eden	—	—	—	—	—	—	—	14	—	—	—	—	660
Tayport	—	—	—	4	4	8	14	16	—	—	—	—	171
Newburgh	—	1	—	—	—	1	9	4	—	—	—	—	—
Totals	23	60	—	52	28	163	2,799	817	153,629	47,413	14,092	16,738	4,660
Montrose District.													
Dundee	†5	15	—	—	—	20	524	75	415	75	22,999	28,338	—
Broughty Ferry	—	—	—	3	10	13	25	25	30	20	27	10	367
Easthaven	—	—	—	—	1	1	1	2	—	—	—	—	10
Arbroath	—	22	—	8	—	30	396	122	1,029	265	19,685	22,570	1,731
Auchmithie	—	—	—	—	6	6	9	12	—	—	15	9	28
Ferryden .... } Montrose .... }	—	6	—	8	—	14	81	47	116	33	3,482	4,703	1,899
Johnshaven	—	2	—	12	1	15	57	42	3	2	2,288	2,078	794
Gourdon	—	17	—	12	3	32	248	107	—	—	13,508	14,937	760
Totals	†5	62	—	43	21	131	1,341	432	1,593	395	62,004	72,645	5,589

*Drifters or Liners except as distinguished. †Trawlers.

Place.	Fishing Craft. 30 feet keel and upwards.*			Under 30 feet keel.		Total.		Fishermen.	Quantity and Value of Fish Landed by British Vessels. Herrings.		Other kinds (except Shell Fish).		Value of Shell Fish.
	Steam	Motor	Sail	Motor	Sail	No.	Tons	No.	Cwts.	£	Cwts.	£	£
Anstruther District.													
Buckhaven	—	1	—	5	—	6	23	8	—	—	—	—	—
Methil and Leven ...	—	—	—	41	10	51	85	31	—	—	882	2,017	119
Largo	—	—	—	3	1	4	7	7	—	—	3	4	63
Elie and Earlsferry	—	—	—	1	1	2	2	1	—	—	—	—	—
St. Monance	—	10	—	5	2	17	242	92	46	48	4,454	9,047	254
Pittenweem	—	18	—	11	1	30	390	157	17	11	9,173	21,276	469
Anstruther	3	10	—	6	3	22	441	131	32	37	5,642	12,823	1,106
Crail	—	—	—	20	3	23	58	51	—	—	85	155	21,115
St. Andrews	—	—	—	12	1	13	20	16	—	—	27	51	524
Tayport	—	—	—	3	2	5	8	3	—	—	—	—	56
Newburgh	—	3	—	1	—	4	35	10	—	—	102	704	—
Totals	3	42	—	108	24	177	1,311	507	95	96	20,368	46,077	23,706
Montrose District.													
Dundee	†7	7	—	—	—	14	651	83	321	178	28,211	45,541	—
Broughty Ferry	—	1	—	3	—	4	16	6	—	—	—	—	16
Easthaven	—	—	—	—	—	—	—	—	—	—	—	—	—
Arbroath	—	26	—	11	—	37	497	161	—	—	31,121	76,149	8,656
Auchmithie	—	—	—	1	—	1	1	2	—	—	—	—	29
Ferryden }													
Montrose }	—	5	—	14	—	19	92	33	—	—	1,486	4,647	3,432
Johnshaven	—	14	—	11	—	13	50	33	—	—	1,335	3,217	2,572
Gourdon	—	14	—	19	—	33	232	99	—	—	13,003	24,722	3,406
Totals	†7	55	—	59	—	121	1,539	417	321	178	75,156	154,276	18,111

*Drifters or Liners except as distinguished

†Trawlers.

Place.	Fishing Craft. 30 feet keel and upwards.*			Under 30 feet keel.		Total.		Fishermen.	Quantity and Value of Fish Landed by British Vessels. Herrings.		Other kinds (except Shell Fish).		Value of Shell Fish.
	Steam	Motor	Sail	Motor	Sail	No.	Tons	No.	Cwts.	£	Cwts.	£	£
Stonehaven District.													
Catterline	—	—	—	4	1	5	7	10	—	—	54	29	311
Stonehaven	—	1	—	4	18	23	51	37	—	—	3,999	4,098	248
Cowie	—	—	—	—	1	1	2	2	—	—	—	—	—
Skateraw	—	—	—	1	—	1	4	3	—	—	63	43	—
Totals	—	1	—	9	20	30	64	52	—	—	4,116	4,170	559
Aberdeen District													
Downies	—	—	—	1	1	2	2	4	—	—	—	—	56
Portlethen	—	—	—	1	4	5	7	10	—	—	—	—	56
Cove	—	—	—	1	2	3	5	6	—	—	38	25	54
Aberdeen	{†253 ‡26}	4	—	30	5	318	24,447	2,836	190,812	71,405	1,607,683	1,761,985	93
Totals	279	4	—	33	12	328	24,461	2,856	190,812	71,405	1,607,721	1,762,010	259
Peterhead District.													
Newburgh	—	—	—	—	1	1	1	2	—	—	—	—	320
Collieston	—	—	—	—	10	10	7	8	—	—	413	214	—
Whinnyfold	3	—	—	4	—	7	122	12	—	—	368	355	39
Port Erroll	—	—	—	4	1	5	23	20	—	—	300	414	—
Boddam	3	2	—	7	12	24	172	80	—	—	49	31	159
Peterhead	82	20	—	56	23	181	3,573	762	304,885	106,085	14,472	10,362	458
Rattray	—	—	—	1	1	2	2	2	—	—	4	2	51
Totals	88	22	—	72	48	230	3,900	886	304,885	106,085	15,606	11,378	1,027

*Drifters or Liners except as distinguished. †Trawlers. ‡Liners.

Place.	Fishing Craft. 30 feet keel and upwards.* Steam	Motor	Sail	Under 30 feet keel. Motor	Sail	Total. No.	Tons	Fishermen. No.	Quantity and Value of Fish Landed by British Vessels. Herrings. Cwts.	£	Other kinds (except Shell Fish). Cwts.	£	Value of Shell Fish. £
Stonehaven District.													
Catterline	—	—	—	8	—	8	14	15	—	—	301	487	3,483
Stonehaven	—	5	—	19	24	48	120	68	—	—	5,942	12,912	3,555
Cowie	—	—	—	—	1	1	1	1	—	—	—	—	—
Skateraw	—	—	—	—	5	5	3	5	—	—	—	—	—
Totals	—	5	—	27	30	62	138	89	—	—	6,243	13,399	7,038
Aberdeen District.													
Downies	—	—	—	2	3	5	3	6	—	—	—	—	—
Portlethen	—	—	—	—	5	5	3	5	—	—	—	—	—
Cove	—	—	—	2	2	4	5	10	—	—	49	68	576
Aberdeen	13 ‡22 †171	22 ‡4 †2	—	30	—	264	18,858	2,562	264,049	321,041	1,735,307	4,263,575	96
Totals	206	28	—	34	10	278	18,869	2,583	264,049	321,041	1,735,356	4,263,643	672
Peterhead District.													
Newburgh	—	—	—	—	—	—	—	—	—	—	—	—	—
Collieston	—	—	—	4	7	11	9	12	—	—	468	853	15
Whinnyfold	—	—	—	3	1	4	7	9	—	—	6	10	6
Port Erroll	—	3	—	5	4	12	39	27	—	—	1,402	4,165	—
Boddam	—	3	—	15	2	20	81	41	—	—	23	41	1,571
Peterhead	†2 88	49	—	37	7	183	5,216	964	377,910	415,064	179,553	358,801	2,480
Totals	90	55	—	64	21	230	5,352	1,053	377,910	415,064	181,452	363,870	4,072

*Drifters or Liners except as distinguished. †Trawlers. ‡Liners.

Place.	Fishing Craft. 30 feet keel and upwards.*			Under 30 feet keel.		Total.		Fishermen.	Quantity and Value of Fish Landed by British Vessels. Herrings.		Other kinds (except Shell Fish).		Value of Shell Fish.
	Steam	Motor	Sail	Motor	Sail	No.	Tons	No.	Cwts.	£	Cwts.	£	£
Fraserburgh District.													
St Combs and Charleston	16	—	—	5	21	42	626	156	—	—	207	121	820
Inverallochy	14	—	—	23	4	41	610	163					
Cairnbulg	9	3	—	20	8	40	540	173	—	—	3	2	136
Fraserburgh	31	34	—	40	11	116	2,382	562	441,392	170,737	42,374	35,852	442
Sandhaven and Pitullie	—	—	—	3	11	14	27	19	—	—	407	239	318
Rosehearty	8	4	—	11	16	39	569	142	—	—	5,417	3,033	131
Pennan	1	—	—	8	3	12	43	29	—	—	1,768	614	360
Totals	79	41	—	110	74	304	4,797	1,244	441,392	170,737	50,176	39,861	2,207
Banff District.													
Crovie	—	—	—	3	20	23	34	18	—	—	—	—	—
Gardenstown	19	9	—	5	10	43	1,089	285	—	—	1,093	595	318
Macduff	11	36	—	3	6	56	925	209	17,616	6,982	20,665	29,326	260
Banff	1	6	—	3	7	17	115	42	—	—	—	—	—
Whitehills	2	35	—	13	1	51	557	171	—	—	18,459	26,446	167
Portsoy	3	—	—	7	25	35	171	83	—	—	732	449	27
Sandend	1	—	—	9	6	16	70	42	—	—	235	91	—
Totals	37	86	—	43	75	241	2,961	850	17,616	6,982	41,184	56,907	772

*Drifters or Liners except as distinguished.

Place.	Fishing Craft.								Quantity and Value of Fish Landed by British Vessels.				
	30 feet keel and upwards.*			Under 30 feet keel		Total.		Fisher-men.	Herrings.		Other kinds (except Shell Fish).		Value of Shell Fish.
	Steam	Motor	Sail	Motor	Sail	No.	Tons	No.	Cwts.	£	Cwts.	£	£
Fraserburgh District.													
St. Combs and Charleston	7	1	—	13	5	26	340	130	—	—	214	404	940
Inverallochy	6	1	—	12	1	20	320	118	—	—	65	123	333
Cairnbulg	3	1	—	8	6	18	187	117	—	—	—	—	—
Fraserburgh	15	60	—	31	7	113	3,008	598	556,660	601,986	143,623	280,648	27,235
Sandhaven and Pitullie	—	—	—	7	4	11	28	25	—	—	251	458	2,311
Rosehearty	4	9	—	15	5	33	489	140	—	—	3,159	5,474	789
Pennan	—	—	—	12	6	18	20	26	—	—	2,086	3,690	1,001
Totals	35	72	—	98	34	239	4,392	1,154	556,660	601,986	149,398	290,797	32,609
Banff District.													
Crovie	—	—	—	5	9	14	21	19	—	—	—	—	—
Gardenstown	19	16	—	13	6	54	1,416	390	24	33	8,325	11,022	1,087
Macduff	2	34	—	5	3	44	687	223	1,186	1,517	32,965	74,365	76
Banff	—	1	—	4	3	8	22	11	—	—	—	—	—
Whitehills	—	31	—	5	5	41	489	160	—	—	12,687	32,251	831
Portsoy	1	3	—	29	7	40	186	89	—	—	4,075	4,585	1,063
Sandend	—	1	—	8	1	10	36	22	—	—	842	873	852
Totals	22	86	—	69	34	211	2,857	914	1,210	1,550	58,894	123,096	3,909

*Drifters or Liners except as distinguished.

Place.	Fishing Craft. 30 feet keel and upwards.*			Under 30 feet keel.		Total.		Fishermen.	Quantity and Value of Fish Landed by British Vessels. Herrings.		Other kinds (except Shell Fish).		Value of Shell Fish.
	Steam	Motor	Sail	Motor	Sail	No.	Tons	No.	Cwts.	£	Cwts.	£	£
Buckie District.													
Cullen	9	10	—	1	6	26	473	154	18	5	165	107	—
Portknockie	19	4	—	9	18	50	784	284	4	2	4,162	6,506	3
Findochty	13	16	—	8	10	47	1,131	304	—	—	1,101	841	—
Portessie	8	3	—	—	—	11	406	95	—	—	—	—	—
Buckie	{†2} {53}	11	—	7	11	84	2,409	599	5,179	1,566	4,027	6,553	—
Portgordon	13	—	—	—	8	21	458	133	—	—	126	104	154
Totals	117	44	—	25	53	239	5,661	1,569	5,201	1,573	9,581	14,111	157
Findhorn Disrict.													
Lossiemouth	4	81	—	6	—	91	2,226	468	64	23	101,709	126,977	365
Hopeman	8	14	—	2	3	27	620	192	—	—	97	212	107
Burghead	9	4	—	1	—	14	417	152	101	32	963	1,315	11
Findhorn	—	—	—	—	—	—	—	—	—	—	—	—	1
Nairn	6	10	—	3	—	19	506	142	238	70	424	533	12
Campbeltown	—	—	—	3	2	5	16	19	—	—	92	96	—
Inverness	—	—	—	—	—	—	—	—	23,487	4,613	129	165	—
Totals	27	109	—	15	5	156	3,785	973	23,890	4,738	103,414	129,298	496

*Drifters or Liners except as distinguished. †Trawlers.

Place.	Fishing Craft. 30 feet keel and upwards.*			Under 30 feet keel.		Total.		Fishermen.	Quantity and Value of Fish Landed by British Vessels. Herrings.		Other kinds (except Shell Fish).		Value of Shell Fish.
	Steam	Motor	Sail	Motor	Sail	No.	Tons	No.	Cwts.	£	Cwts.	£	£
Buckie District.													
Cullen	—	7	—	7	7	21	182	43	—	—	257	222	—
Portknockie	13	6	—	13	3	35	692	214	—	—	876	1,670	122
Findochty	6	12	—	11	4	33	740	173	—	—	315	564	—
Portessie	1	4	—	—	—	5	194	50	—	—	—	—	—
Buckie	24	31	—	5	8	68	2,027	540	10,429	11,948	61,224	150,073	885
Portgordon	4	8	—	3	3	18	389	133	—	—	—	—	532
Totals	48	68	—	39	25	180	4,224	1,153	10,429	11,948	62,672	152,529	1,539
Findhorn District.													
Lossiemouth	1	70	—	4	—	75	2,035	397	290	95	69,792	191,330	580
Hopeman	—	18	—	7	2	27	533	182	—	—	238	588	285
Burghead	1	9	—	1	—	11	390	110	—	—	4,428	11,057	478
Findhorn	—	—	—	—	—	—	—	—	—	—	—	—	—
Nairn	—	9	—	3	—	12	294	83	1,593	1,214	337	928	390
Campbeltown	—	—	—	—	—	—	—	—	—	—	—	—	—
Inverness	—	—	—	—	—	—	—	—	10,314	7,876	—	—	—
Totals	2	106	—	15	2	125	3,252	772	12,197	9,185	74,795	203,903	1,733

*Drifters or Liners except as distinguished.

Place.	Fishing Craft. 30 feet keel and upwards.*			Under 30 feet keel.		Total.		Fishermen.	Quantity and Value of Fish Landed by British Vessels. Herrings.		Other kinds (except Shell Fish).		Value of Shell Fish.
	Steam	Motor	Sail	Motor	Sail	No.	Tons	No.	Cwts.	£	Cwts.	£	£
Cromarty District.													
Avoch	—	12	—	11	4	27	293	185	—	—	159	193	—
Cromarty to Saltburn	—	—	—	—	12	12	20	12	56	15	666	552	85
Shandwick to Hilton	—	—	—	7	—	7	27	12	—	—	387	475	65
Rockfield and Portmahomack	—	—	—	3	3	6	16	10	35	11	231	354	426
Totals	—	12	—	21	19	52	356	219	91	26	1,443	1,574	576
Helmsdale District.													
Embo	—	—	—	2	2	4	7	14	—	—	335	331	72
Golspie	—	2	—	5	—	7	51	14	—	—	1,658	1,892	29
Brora	—	1	—	7	2	10	32	12	—	—	828	930	179
Helmsdale	—	17	—	8	2	27	247	83	84	14	13,136	15,166	507
Dunbeath	—	4	—	4	1	9	71	16	—	—	1,686	2,177	90
Totals	—	24	—	26	7	57	408	139	84	14	17,643	20,496	877
Lybster District.													
Latheronwheel	—	—	—	1	4	5	10	9	—	—	13	8	39
Forse	—	—	—	—	1	1	2	4	}				
Lybster	—	6	—	6	2	14	97	45	—	—	2,923	4,776	102
Totals	—	6	—	7	7	20	109	‡58	—	—	2,936	4,784	141

*Drifters or Liners except as distinguished.

‡Including 17 crofter fishermen.

Place.	Fishing Craft. 30 feet keel and upwards.*			Under 30 feet keel.		Total.		Fishermen.	Quantity and Value of Fish Landed by British Vessels. Herrings.		Other kinds (except Shell Fish).		Value of Shell Fish.
	Steam	Motor	Sail	Motor	Sail	No.	Tons	No.	Cwts.	£	Cwts.	£	£
Cromarty District.													
Avoch	—	13	—	6	—	19	281	113	—	—	18	36	3
Cromarty to Saltburn	—	2	—	2	2	6	69	4	—	—	177	289	28
Sandwick to Hilton	—	—	—	2	—	2	5	—	—	—	—	—	—
Rockfield and Portmahomack	—	2	—	4	—	6	49	7	—	—	126	608	474
Totals	—	17	—	14	2	33	404	124	—	—	321	933	505
Helmsdale District.													
Embo	—	—	—	—	—	—	—	—	—	—	—	—	6
Golspie	—	5	—	2	—	7	70	15	—	—	1,405	3,997	253
Brora	—	3	—	6	1	10	47	14	—	—	552	1,300	830
Helmsdale	—	16	—	7	1	24	269	77	—	—	8,903	30,863	3,357
Dunbeath	—	5	—	6	—	11	77	23	—	—	2,433	6,711	618
Totals	—	29	—	21	2	52	463	129	—	—	13,293	42,871	5,064
Lybster District.													
Latheronwheel	—	—	—	2	1	3	4	5	—	—	—	—	392
Lybster	—	8	—	6	—	14	96	42	311	339	4,734	15,154	448
Clyth	—	—	—	2	1	3	4	6	—	—	—	—	451
Totals	—	8	—	10	2	20	104	‡53	311	339	4,734	15,154	1,291

*Drifters or Liners except as distinguished

‡Including 6 crofter fishermen.

Place.	Fishing Craft. 30 feet keel and upwards.*			Under 30 feet keel.		Total.		Fishermen.	Quantity and Value of Fish Landed by British Vessels. Herrings.		Other kinds (except Shell Fish).		Value of Shell Fish.
	Steam	Motor	Sail	Motor	Sail	No.	Tons	No.	Cwts.	£	Cwts.	£	£
Wick District.													
Whaligoe and Sarclet	—	—	—	1	4	5	10	14	—	—	7	5	102
Wick	5	19	—	11	2	37	610	125	102,176	43,055	19,339	25,498	167
Boathaven and Staxigoe	—	1	—	5	—	6	24	15	—	—	151	218	11
Ackergill	—	—	—	—	—	3	7	7	—	—	642	772	41
Keiss and Nybster	—	2	—	9	—	11	56	24	—	—	1,240	1,642	1,087
Auckengill and Freswick	—	1	—	3	15	19	46	22	—	—	300	202	—
Stroma	—	—	—	18	8	26	58	42	—	—	348	174	504
Duncansby and Huna	—	—	—	6	7	13	23	31	—	—	85	57	453
Gills and Mey	—	—	—	3	12	15	29	28					
Scarfskerry and Ham	—	—	—	1	5	6	12	14	—	—	196	103	243
Brough and Dunnet	—	—	—	2	10	12	24	16					
Castehill and Murkle	—	—	—	1	—	1	2	2	—	—	20	13	61
Thurso and Scrabster	—	5	—	12	5	22	110	73	1,043	366	10,049	13,596	413
Crosskirk and Brims	—	—	—	—	3	3	6	5	—	—	—	—	45
Sandside	—	—	—	2	—	2	5	5	—	—	157	95	172
Portskerra	—	—	—	6	7	13	27	36	14	8	946	893	167
Strathypoint and Armadale	—	—	—	1	8	9	19	27					
Kirtomy and Farr...	—	—	—	—	4	4	8	22	—	—	28	20	165
Skerray	—	—	—	2	2	4	8	15	—	—	131	144	249
Scullomy	—	—	—	—	1	1	2	2					
Island Roan	—	—	—	1	—	1	2	5	—	—	14	9	76
Talmine and Portvasgo	—	—	—	—	7	7	14	18	—	—	317	231	237
Erribol and Rispond	—	—	—	6	8	14	32	28	—	—	255	370	1,499
Totals	5	28	—	93	108	234	1,134	†576	103,233	43,429	34,225	44,042	5,692

* Drifters or Liners. †Including 241 crofter fishermen.

Place.	Fishing Craft. 30 feet keel and upwards.*			Under 30 feet keel.		Total.		Fishermen.	Quantity and Value of Fish Landed by British Vessels. Herrings.		Other kinds (except Shell Fish).		Value of Shell Fish.
	Steam	Motor	Sail	Motor	Sail	No.	Tons	No.	Cwts.	£	Cwts.	£	£
Wick District.													
Whaligoe and Sarclet	—	—	—	3	3	6	8	8	—	—	—	—	294
Wick	—	35	—	10	1	46	849	162					
Boathaven and Staxigoe	—	—	—	4	—	4	16	9	40,224	40,484	44,475	115,477	1,622
Ackergill	—	—	—	3	1	4	8	6	—	—	250	927	605
Keiss and Nybster	—	—	—	6	—	6	20	24					
Auckengill and Freswick	—	—	—	3	5	8	12	9	—	—	42	81	10,967
Stroma	—	—	—	19	3	22	44	28	—	—	36	153	3,196
Duncansby and Huna	—	—	—	6	7	13	18	14	—	—	108	204	836
Gills and Mey	—	—	—	3	2	5	9	6					
Scarfskerry and Ham	—	—	—	8	1	9	17	10	—	—	138	267	1,391
Brough and Dunnet	—	—	—	13	1	14	25	18					
Castlehill and Murkle	—	—	—	1	—	1	2	2					
Thurso and Scrabster	—	17	—	11	1	29	470	92	10,730	11,720	52,843	138,243	615
Crosskirk and Brims	—	—	—	2	—	2	2	4					
Sandside	—	—	—	2	1	3	5	4					
Portskerra, Strathy-point and Armadale	—	—	—	12	17	29	54	54	35	45	146	272	1,127
Kirtomy and Farr	—	—	—	1	3	4	6	6	—	—	—		200
Skerray, Scullomy,	—	—	—	8	—	8	11	15	—	—	10	24	1,545
Talmine and Portvasgo	—	—	—	6	2	8	7	14	—	—	—	—	1,021
Erribol and Rispond	—	—	—	10	6	16	29	19	—	—	26	60	1,219
Totals	—	52	—	131	54	237	1,612	†504	50,989	52,249	98,074	255,708	24,638

* Drifters or Liners. †Including 178 crofter fishermen.

Place.	Fishing Craft.								Quantity and Value of Fish Landed by British Vessels.				
	30 feet keel and upwards.*			Under 30 feet keel.		Total.		Fishermen.	Herrings.		Other kinds (except Shell Fish).		Value of Shell Fish.
	Steam	Motor	Sail	Motor	Sail	No.	Tons	No.	Cwts.	£	Cwts.	£	£
Orkney District.													
North Ronaldshay ...	—	—	—	1	2	3	6	8					
Sanday	—	—	—	4	28	32	35	52	} —	—	—	—	1,312
Westray and Papa	—	—	—	29	29	58	78	110	—	—	575	515	954
Eday and Pharay ...	—	—	—	10	14	24	29	30	—	—	—	—	450
Stronsay	—	—	—	12	18	30	39	29	54,590	23,293	1,796	246	421
Shapinsay	—	—	—	4	6	10	10	13					
Rousay, Egilshay, &c.	—	—	—	9	10	19	16	19	} —	—	—	—	607
Evie and Birsay ...	—	—	—	13	6	19	21	40	—	—	193	196	643
Kirkwall	—	—	—	12	3	15	43	17	4	2	21	26	225
Tankerness and Deerness	—	—	—	9	3	12	18	12	—	—	147	150	360
Holm	—	—	—	4	2	6	9	10	7	3	89	86	88
Burray	—	2	—	6	6	14	103	19	—	—	—	—	70
Orphir to Scapa ...	—	—	—	2	2	4	7	6	—	—	—	—	135
Stromness	—	—	—	25	3	28	46	31	—	—	1,024	977	674
Hoy and Graemsay	—	—	—	20	3	23	31	26	—	—	192	191	770
Walls	—	—	—	20	7	27	48	38					
Flotta	—	—	—	1	4	5	7	6	} —	—	76	99	734
Phara and Cava......	—	—	—	2	—	2	2	4					
Swona	—	—	—	1	—	1	2	3	} 3	2	87	107	483
South Ronaldshay...	—	—	—	20	21	41	58	41					
Totals	—	2	—	204	167	373	608	‡514	54,604	23,300	4,200	2,593	7,926

*Drifters or Liners.

‡Including 388 crofter fishermen.

Place.	30 feet keel and upwards.*			Under 30 feet keel.		Total.		Fishermen.	Herrings.		Other kinds (except Shell Fish).		Value of Shell Fish.
	Steam	Motor	Sail	Motor	Sail	No.	Tons	No.	Cwts.	£	Cwts.	£	£
Orkney District.													
North Ronaldshay ..	—	—	—	14	9	23	22	27	—	—	—	—	—
Sanday	—	—	—	18	42	60	58	67	—	—	8	20	10,404
Westray and Papa	—	—	—	50	43	93	109	106	—	—	47	121	7,707
Eday and Pharay ...	—	—	—	22	16	38	43	51	—	—	12	37	3,710
Stronsay	—	—	—	22	18	40	47	46	—	—	—	—	6,762
Shapinshay	—	—	—	8	15	23	24	29	—	—	—	—	5,570
Rousay, Egilshay, &c.	—	—	—	19	8	27	25	34	—	—	—	—	—
Evie and Birsay ...	—	—	—	20	4	24	26	30	—	—	—	—	3,382
Kirkwall	—	—	—	26	10	36	58	39	—	—	102	219	4,776
Tankerness and Deerness	—	—	—	13	5	18	22	26	—	—	122	275	2,342
Holm	—	1	—	4	9	14	20	15	—	—	20	30	1,454
Burray	—	—	—	9	6	15	18	18	—	—	—	—	879
Orphir to Scapa ...	—	—	—	4	4	8	7	11	—	—	—	—	2,272
Stromness	—	—	—	35	—	35	68	33	—	—	387	955	4,338
Hoy and Graemsay	—	—	—	20	1	21	31	32	—	—	30	68	9,564
Walls	—	1	—	20	5	26	54	39	—	—	39	67	4,012
Flotta	—	—	—	5	—	5	8	8	—	—	—	—	—
Phara and Cava ...	—	—	—	2	—	2	2	2	—	—	—	—	—
Swona	—	—	—	1	—	1	2	2	—	—	—	—	—
South Ronaldshay ..	—	—	—	28	27	55	70	59	—	—	18	38	2,002
Totals	—	2	—	340	222	564	714	‡674	—	—	785	1,830	69,174

* Drifters or Liners.

‡Including 435 crofter fishermen.

Place.	Fishing Craft. 30 feet keel and upwards.*			Under 30 feet keel.		Total.		Fishermen.	Quantity and Value of Fish Landed by British Vessels. Herrings.		Other kinds (except Shell Fish).		Value of Shell Fish.
	Steam	Motor	Sail	Motor	Sail	No.	Tons	No.	Cwts.	£	Cwts.	£	£
Shetland District.													
Dunrossness, Fair Isle	—	3	—	2	20	25	152	83	—	—	183	91	—
Levenwick, Hoswick	—	3	—	1	16	20	171	50	—	—	400	219	3
Sandsair, Aithsvoe	—	—	—	1	1	2	5	4	—	—	—	—	—
Lerwick, Bressay ...	4	14	—	11	14	43	445	86	583,789	219,170	20,266	13,429	515
Whalsay, Skerries .	2	12	1	9	4	28	578	78	11,242	4,262	4,845	3,171	—
Yell and Fetlar	—	—	—	2	—	2	6	5	3,374	1,269	108	41	6
Uyasound	—	—	—	—	1	1	1	—	—	—	—	—	—
Baltasound	—	—	—	—	7	7	10	5	3	1	109	55	—
North Roe, Yell Sound	—	—	—	1	7	8	9	7	—	—	—	—	—
Ronasvoe and Hillswick	—	—	—	3	24	27	30	22	—	—	—	—	—
Walls, Sandness and Foula	—	1	—	13	31	45	79	28	—	—	—	—	—
Scalloway and Isles	5	35	1	22	24	87	1,552	270	1,383	543	6,613	5,085	917
Totals	11	68	2	65	149	295	3,038	†638	599,791	225,245	32,524	22,091	1,441
Stornoway District.													
South Lochs	—	16	—	11	18	45	460	163	175	42	88	70	197
North Lochs	—	2	—	4	31	37	141	155	74	23	750	421	33
Stornoway	5	1	—	6	7	19	259	89	190,893	96,237	12,549	6,429	70
Garrabost	—	8	2	—	19	29	475	216	—	—	1,145	635	379
Portnaguran	—	2	—	3	19	24	141	154	—	—	344	383	135
Back	—	4	—	—	27	31	236	207	—	—	2,851	2,868	—
Ness	—	—	—	—	17	17	52	108	241	103	826	819	—

*Drifters or Liners

†Including 388 crofter fishermen.

Place.	Fishing Craft. 30 feet keel and upwards.*			Under 30 feet keel.		Total.		Fishermen.	Quantity and Value of Fish Landed by British Vessels. Herrings.		Other kinds (except Shell Fish).		Value of Shell Fish.
	Steam	Motor	Sail	Motor	Sail	No.	Tons	No.	Cwts.	£	Cwts.	£	£
Shetland District.													
Dunrossness, Fair Isle	—	3	—	10	13	26	210	42	—	—	86	205	884
Levenwick, Hoswick	—	—	—	2	9	11	18	9	—	—	19	26	274
Sandsair, Aithsvoe	—	—	—	4	5	10	29	12	—	—	69	180	268
Lerwick, Bressay	2	24	1	15	9	51	838	154	483,064	409,690	17,374	42,143	543
Whalsay, Skerries	—	13	—	9	4	26	454	130	7,858	6,732	10,077	24,299	121
Yell and Fetlar	—	2	—	11	3	16	52	14	3,513	2,997	857	1,848	69
Uyasound	—	—	—	2	—	2	3	5	—	—	181	358	31
Baltasound	—	—	—	3	4	7	16	10	—	—	105	206	41
North Roe, Yellsound	—	—	—	6	5	11	18	8	—	—	31	44	136
Ronasvoe and Hillswick	—	—	—	6	10	16	20	10	—	—	31	46	61
Walls, Sandness and Foula	—	2	—	18	11	31	108	18	—	—	5,774	13,164	853
Scalloway and Isles	1	38	—	39	16	94	1,322	255	7,847	7,144	18,693	41,777	675
Totals	3	83	1	125	89	301	3,088	†667	502,282	426,563	53,297	124,296	3,956
Stornoway District.													
South Lochs	—	17	—	50	19	86	439	203	381	408	360	501	1,469
North Lochs	—	3	—	35	23	61	141	186	3,327	3,828	260	350	477
Stornoway	13	15	—	50	5	83	1,033	303	247,544	261,514	2,241	3,277	63
Garrabost	—	5	—	11	12	28	261	105	—	—	611	1,209	880
Portnaguran	—	2	—	12	8	22	63	97	49	24	2,355	4,706	624
Back	—	2	—	11	21	34	158	142	—	—	1,622	3,248	—
Ness	—	—	—	13	7	20	42	89	—	—	772	1,256	—

* Drifters or Liners.

†Including 83 crofter fishermen.

Place.	Fishing Craft. 30 feet keel and upwards.* Steam	Motor	Sail	Under 30 feet keel. Motor	Sail	Total. No.	Tons	Fishermen. No.	Quantity and Value of Fish Landed by British Vessels. Herrings. Cwts.	£	Other kinds (except Shell Fish). Cwts.	£	Value of Shell Fish. £
Stornoway District.—Contd.													
Shawbost	—	—	—	1	7	8	17	41	—	—	348	203	99
Carloway	—	1	—	—	9	10	50	40	35	8	540	285	177
Bernera	—	1	—	2	30	33	110	114	—	—	190	110	589
Valtos	—	—	—	3	3	6	20	25	35	8	378	215	190
North Harris	—	4	—	11	38	53	178	195	722	253	711	744	1,398
Scalpay	—	14	—	12	23	49	314	189	2,250	1,297	433	223	1,257
South Harris	—	—	—	10	39	49	105	149	—	—	5,530	1,555	1,927
Totals	5	53	2	63	287	410	2,558	‡1,845	194,425	97,971	26,683	14,960	6,451
Barra District.													
Bernera	—	1	—	21	7	29	125	27	—	—	55	11	1,340
Hougharry and Loch Eport	—	—	—	13	16	29	56	30	}				
Grimsay	—	—	—	18	32	50	97	38	}				
Heisker	—	—	—	—	1	1	2	2	} 39	8	82	37	1,545
Benbecula	—	—	—	7	21	28	49	33	}				
Loch Carnan	—	—	—	7	24	31	59	24	522	158	230	78	686
Loch Skipport	—	—	—	4	8	12	22	11	—	—	—	—	58
Loch Boisdale	—	2	—	10	46	58	182	99	2,496	707	418	599	1,523
Eriskay	—	9	—	6	23	38	261	71	42	9	75	75	103
Bruernish	—	2	—	14	36	52	140	44 }					
Ault and Earsary ...	—	—	—	—	3	3	5	5 }					
Brevig and Skallary	—	—	—	—	7	7	10	7 }	31,479	19,961	2,848	521	1,519
Castlebay	—	4	—	5	23	32	121	46 }					
Sold at Sea	—	—	—	—	—	—	—	—	3,210	775	—	—	—
Totals	—	18	—	105	247	370	1,129	§437	37,788	21,618	3,708	1,321	6,774

*Drifters or Liners. ‡Including 1,791 crofter fishermen. §All crofter fishermen.

Place.	Fishing Craft. 30 feet keel and upwards.* Steam	Motor	Sail	Under 30 feet keel. Motor	Sail	Total. No.	Tons	Fishermen. No.	Quantity and Value of Fish Landed by British Vessels. Herrings. Cwts.	£	Other kinds (except Shell Fish). Cwts.	£	Value of Shell Fish. £
Stornoway District. (Contd.)													
Shawbost	—	—	—	6	1	7	8	22	—	—	60	74	60
Carloway	—	—	—	9	5	14	28	40	—	—	139	174	—
Bernera	—	—	—	34	6	40	68	84	—	—	5	7	2,841
Valtos	—	—	—	16	7	23	44	44	—	—	78	98	110
North Harris	—	2	—	36	37	75	167	207	11,948	12,228	—	—	2,892
Scalpay	—	14	—	29	20	63	346	150	28	24	269	393	2,025
South Harris	—	3	—	32	38	73	184	195	—	—	425	335	5,435
Totals	13	63	—	344	209	629	2,982	‡1,867	263,277	278,026	9,197	15,628	16,876
Barra District.													
Bernera	—	1	—	20	3	24	87	51	—	—	8	12	5,110
Hougharry and Loch Eport	—	—	—	26	6	32	60	59					
Grimsay	—	—	—	30	9	39	78	67	140	180	—	—	8,986
Benbecula	—	—	—	17	10	27	46	43					
Loch Carnan	—	—	—	13	6	19	32	35	315	265	75	80	1,359
Loch Skipport	—	—	—	7	3	10	19	8	210	180	—	—	768
Loch Boisdale	—	1	—	16	29	46	114	96	5,905	5,740	306	1,364	2,646
Eriskay	—	2	—	3	15	20	70	48	140	100	—	—	1,255
Bruernish	—	2	—	18	20	40	123	83					
Ault and Earsary	—	—	—	2	2	4	7	12	6,632	5,937	140	338	17,572
Brevig and Skallary	—	—	—	2	1	3	4	9					
Castlebay	—	1	—	27	17	45	115	99					
Sold at Sea	—	—	—	—	—	—	—	—	508	580	—	—	—
Totals	—	7	—	181	121	309	755	§610	13,850	12,982	529	1,794	37,696

* Drifters or Liners. ‡Including 1,538 crofter fishermen. §Including 570 crofter fishermen.

Place.	Fishing Craft. 30 feet keel and upwards.			Under 30 feet keel.		Total.		Fishermen.	Quantity and Value of Fish Landed by British Vessels. Herrings.		Other kinds (except Shell Fish).		Value of Shell Fish.
	Steam	Motor	Sail	Motor	Sail	No.	Tons	No.	Cwts.	£	Cwts.	£	£
Loch Broom District.													
Poulin to Ardmore	—	—	—	3	32	35	86	38	—	—	—	—	316
Findlemore to Badcall	—	—	—	7	16	23	42	29	—	—	1	1	836
Unapool to Ned	—	—	—	3	4	7	15	11	—	—	101	83	810
Drumbeg to Achnacarion	—	—	—	3	6	9	18	15	—	—	25	17	36
Culkein to Inverkirkaig	—	—	—	5	14	19	39	30	733	177	—	—	134
Achnahaird to Culnacraig	—	—	—	3	11	14	37	22	—	—	2	2	384
Islemartin to Logie	—	—	—	7	30	37	77	32	181	50	522	381	162
Auchmore to Badlurach	—	—	—	1	3	4	7	6	—	—	38	32	180
First Coast to Aultbea	—	—	—	1	12	13	19	16	—	—	97	65	—
Poolewe to Cove	—	—	—	4	13	17	30	23	—	—	220	163	9
Melvaig to Charlestown	—	—	—	2	10	12	30	17	—	—	560	387	94
Badachro to Red Point	—	—	—	9	2	11	49	28	34	16	1,817	741	137
Totals	—	—	—	48	153	201	449	†267	948	243	3,383	1,872	3,098

†Including 244 crofter fishermen.

Place.	Fishing Craft. 30 feet keel and upwards.			Under 30 feet keel.		Total.		Fishermen.	Quantity and Value of Fish Landed by British Vessels. Herrings.		Other kinds (except Shell Fish).		Value of Shell Fish.
	Steam	Motor	Sail	Motor	Sail	No.	Tons	No.	Cwts.	£	Cwts.	£	£
Loch Broom District.													
Poulin to Ardmore	—	2	—	21	12	35	89	30	4,703	4,032	13,348	31,253	1,683
Findlemore to Badcall	—	1	—	9	9	19	46	18	—	—	40	96	2,048
Unapool to Ned ...	—	—	—	3	2	5	7	4	—	—	25	54	1,040
Drumbeg to Achnacarion	—	1	—	10	2	13	31	14	—	—	—	—	717
Culkein to Inverkirkaig	—	—	—	16	8	24	57	20	3,629	3,652	3,058	6,523	916
Achnahaird to Culnacraig	—	1	—	13	5	19	48	17	—	—	—	—	612
Islemartin to Logie	—	3	—	16	10	29	83	20	174,140	181,396	5,467	6,649	1,830
Achmore to Badlurach	—	—	—	2	3	5	7	4	—	—	5	12	420
First Coast to Aultbea	—	—	—	5	8	13	22	7	—	—	—	—	73
Poolewe to Cove ...	—	—	—	8	8	16	22	9	—	—	33	73	356
Melvaig to Charlestown .... } Baddachro to Red Point .... }	—	2	—	16	6	24	109	30	105,153	125,526	5,273	8,428	646
Totals	—	10	—	119	73	202	521	†173	287,625	314,606	27,249	53,088	10,341

†Including 144 crofter fishermen.

Place.	Fishing Craft. 30 feet keel and upwards. Steam	Motor	Sail	Under 30 feet keel. Motor	Sail	Total. No.	Tons	Fishermen. No.	Quantity and Value of Fish Landed by British Vessels. Herrings. Cwts.	£	Other kinds (except Shell Fish). Cwts.	£	Value of Shell Fish. £
Loch Carron and Skye District.													
Loch Torridon	—	1	—	9	1	11	63	35	125	37	353	852	24
Applecross	—	3	—	8	—	11	115	42	24	7	317	384	12
Kishorn	—	—	—	6	—	6	37	20	188	76	728	382	11
Loch Carron	—	3	—	5	—	8	72	24					
Loch Alsh	—	1	—	2	—	3	24	6	21,701	7,676	3,568	3,589	194
Loch Hourn	—	—	—	1	2	3	5	4					
Sleat	—	—	—	7	—	7	21	17	168	48	248	171	92
Kyleakin	—	3	—	10	1	14	95	29					
Broadford	—	—	—	2	1	3	8	5	255	103	159	203	273
Scalpay Sound	—	—	—	1	19	20	27	27					
Sconcer and Braes	—	—	—	—	9	9	14	17	48	17	16	10	189
Portree	—	4	—	7	10	21	126	47	610	313	276	234	703
Staffin	—	3	—	1	18	22	72	53					
Loch Snizort	—	1	—	7	9	17	63	51	—	—	111	57	250
Waternish	—	2	—	3	3	8	45	16					
Dunvegan	—	—	—	6	9	15	23	20	—	—	77	56	426
Glendale and Bracadale	—	—	—	5	15	20	52	51	21	6	85	70	344
Strathaird	—	—	—	4	1	5	20	7					
Lochs Slapin and Eyshort	—	—	—	2	1	3	5	7	1,019	263	253	91	136
Isle of Soay	—	1	—	6	1	8	20	16	—	—	—	—	253
Totals	—	22	—	92	100	214	907	‡494	24,159	8,546	6,191	6,099	2,907

‡ Including 447 crofter fishermen.

Place.	Fishing Craft. 30 feet keel and upwards. Steam	Motor	Sail	Under 30 feet keel. Motor	Sail	Total. No.	Tons	Fishermen. No.	Quantity and Value of Fish Landed by British Vessels. Herrings. Cwts.	£	Other kinds (except Shell Fish). Cwts.	£	Value of Shell Fish. £
Loch Carron and Skye District.													
Loch Torridon	—	2	—	25	3	30	108	77	43	40	325	592	1,076
Applecross	—	3	—	11	—	14	110	43	14	14	238	415	484
Kishorn	—	1	—	6	—	7	32	16	28	34	913	1,750	489
Loch Carron	—	3	—	14	—	17	102	40					
Loch Alsh	—	1	—	16	—	17	58	20	23,158	29,465	4,183	9,994	660
Loch Hourn	—	—	—	12	1	13	15	18					
Sleat	—	1	—	6	1	8	20	14	—	—	140	247	560
Kyleakin	—	4	—	5	1	10	84	28					
Broadford	—	1	—	4	1	6	11	12	23	23	191	356	1,530
Scalpay Sound	—	—	—	4	10	14	23	25					
Sconcer and Braes	—	1	—	—	10	11	22	30	50	49	80	78	487
Portree	—	1	—	13	10	24	92	68	284	297	902	1,479	8,034
Staffin	—	1	—	1	12	14	36	31					
Loch Snizort	—	—	—	17	13	30	60	52	15	17	207	301	541
Waternish	—	—	—	9	1	10	17	23	69	74	440	833	2,038
Dunvegan	—	—	—	19	6	25	37	49					
Glendale and Bracadale	—	1	—	17	17	35	83	75	—	—	564	681	1,310
Strathaird	—	—	—	7	1	8	20	16					
Lochs Slapin and Eyshort	—	—	—	1	2	3	4	6	—	—	89	119	1,094
Isle of Soay	—	—	—	9	1	10	26	18	35	20	30	40	852
Totals	—	20	—	196	90	306	960	‡661	23,719	30,033	8,302	16,885	19,155

‡Including 571 crofter fishermen.

Place.	Fishing Craft.							Fishermen.	Quantity and Value of Fish Landed by British Vessels.				
	30 feet keel and upwards.			Under 30 feet keel.		Total.			Herrings.		Other kinds (except Shell Fish).		Value of Shell Fish.
	Steam	Motor	Sail	Motor	Sail	No.	Tons	No.	Cwts.	£	Cwts.	£	£
Fort William District.													
Loch Nevis, Mallaig and Morar	—	8	—	11	3	22	133	45	72,709	37,409	8,237	7,960	810
Arisaig and Aylort	—	—	—	3	1	4	6	7	—	—	315	200	332
Smearisary to Ockle Point	—	—	—	2	—	2	12	7	—	—	151	200	—
Ockle Point to Loch Aline	—	—	—	1	8	9	14	13	—	—	857	70	74
North and South Corran to Fort William	—	—	—	2	10	12	15	16	182	106	497	271	—
Loch Leven to Kentallen	—	—	—	1	1	2	7	5	}				
Cuil, Appin and Creran	—	—	—	1	1	2	8	3	214	105	38,810	34,229	150
Loch Etive and Oban	—	1	—	11	1	13	65	14					
Lismore	—	—	—	1	—	1	1	2	}				
Tobermory and Salen	—	—	1	11	2	14	43	14	4	2	253	335	961
Lochs Don, Spelve and Buie	—	—	—	—	1	1	1	2	—	—	54	25	46
Carsaig and Kintra	—	—	—	6	—	6	9	7	7	3	42	12	185
Lochs Laich and Scriddan	—	—	—	5	4	9	17	3	—	—	—	—	—
Ulva, Na Kall and Tuadh	—	—	—	4	5	9	14	9	—	—	—	—	151
Coll	—	—	—	5	6	11	12	14	—	—	—	—	207
Tiree	—	1	—	10	9	20	40	14	—	—	—	—	523
Iona	—	—	—	3	—	3	5	5	—	—	76	60	142

Place.	Fishing Craft. 30 feet keel and upwards. Steam	Motor	Sail	Under 30 feet keel. Motor	Sail	Total. No.	Tons	Fishermen. No.	Quantity and Value of Fish Landed by British Vessels. Herrings. Cwts.	£	Other kinds (except Shell Fish). Cwts.	£	Value of Shell Fish. £
Fort William District.													
Loch Nevis, Mallaig and Morar	—	16	—	21	1	38	360	113	148,796	174,069	10,708	29,922	12,418
Arisaig and Aylort	—	—	—	7	—	7	11	11	—	—	30	31	1,859
Smearisary to Ockle Point	—	—	—	13	—	13	28	7	—	—	—	—	343
Ockle Point to Loch Aline	—	—	—	3	4	7	11	9	—	—	1,056	571	446
North and South Corran to Fort William ..	—	—	—	3	3	6	5	6	32	32	126	117	—
Loch Leven to Kentallan	—	—	—	3	1	4	10	2					
Cull, Appin & Creran	—	—	—	2	—	2	6	3	15,644	16,094	75,530	210,963	3,685
Loch Etive and Oban	—	1	—	8	2	11	40	7					
Lismore	—	—	—	1	—	1	3	2					
Tobermory and Salen	—	—	—	8	—	8	11	11	—	—	100	207	1,254
Lochs Don, Spelve and Buie	—	—	—	1	—	1	1	2	—	—	—	—	172
Carsaig and Kintra	—	—	—	5	1	6	10	8 }					
Lochs Laich and Scriddan	—	—	—	5	1	6	10	7 }	—	—	15	12	620
Ulva, Na Kall and Tuadh	—	—	—	3	—	3	6	5	—	—	—	—	638
Coll	—	1	—	7	4	12	20	13	—	—	—	—	1,994
Tiree	—	—	—	16	4	20	28	37	—	—	—	—	1,492
Iona	—	—	—	4	—	4	8	4	—	—	—	—	90
Canna	—	—	—	5	—	5	16	9	—	—	—	—	865
Rum, Muck and Eigg	—	—	—	2	—	2	2	3	—	—	—	—	545
Totals	—	18	—	117	21	156	586	†259	164,472	190,195	87,565	241,823	26,421

†Including 112 crofter fishermen.

Place.	30 feet keel and upwards. Steam	Motor	Sail	Under 30 feet keel. Motor	Sail	Total. No.	Tons	Fishermen. No.	Herrings. Cwts.	£	Other kinds (except Shell Fish). Cwts.	£	Value of Shell Fish. £
Fort William District. (Contd.)													
Canna	—	—	—	4	—	4	7	7		—	—	—	185
Rum, Muck and Eigg	—	—	—	4	—	4	8	6	—	—	—	—	122
Totals	—	10	1	85	52	148	417	†193	73,116	37,625	49,292	43,362	3,888
Campbeltown District.													
Carradale	—	20	—	5	—	25	421	117	150	47	—	—	13
Campbeltown	—	21	—	22	—	43	539	153	1,587	462	6,866	7,383	469
Sanda	—	1	—	1	—	2	26	3	—	—	—	—	62
Southend	—	—	—	3	—	3	4	4	—	—	—	—	123
Muasdale and Ballochantee	—	—	—	1	3	4	5	5	—	—	—	—	149
Gigha	—	—	—	14	2	16	65	16	—	—	172	172	544
Port Ellen	—	—	—	—	11	11	16	14	—	—	—	—	340
Portaskaig	—	—	—	13	2	15	31	15	—	—	—	—	175
Portnahaven and Port Wemyss	—	—	—	3	6	9	12	9	—	—	12	6	110
Bowmore	—	—	—	—	4	4	5	10	—	—	74	193	—
Port Charlotte	—	—	—	2	6	8	8	8	—	—	126	251	171
Bruichladdich	—	—	—	3	1	4	4	7	—	—	72	143	307
Loch Gruinart	—	—	—	—	—	—	—	—	—	—	59	28	10
Jura	—	—	—	—	4	4	6	4	—	—	—	—	21
Colonsay	—	—	—	3	7	10	10	10	—	—	—	—	176
Sold at Sea	—	—	—	—	—	—	—	—	23,435	5,943	101	29	—
Totals	—	42	—	70	46	158	1,152	‡375	25,172	6,452	7,482	8,205	2,670

†Including 134 crofter fishermen.

‡Including 34 crofter fishermen.

Place.	Fishing Craft. 30 feet keel and upwards. Steam	Motor	Sail	Under 30 feet keel. Motor	Sail	Total. No.	Tons	Fishermen. No.	Quantity and Value of Fish Landed by British Vessels. Herrings. Cwts.	£	Other kinds (except Shell Fish). Cwts.	£	Value of Shell Fish. £
Campbeltown District.													
Carradale	—	14	—	—	—	14	272	84	—	—	—	—	186
Campbeltown	—	23	—	12	1	36	545	179	36,079	37,947	22,772	42,323	2,715
Sanda	—	—	—	1	—	1	2	2	—	—	—	—	196
Southend	—	—	—	4	—	4	5	4	—	—	—	—	335
Muasdale and Ballochantee	—	—	—	3	1	4	3	8	—	—	—	—	1,001
Gigha	—	—	—	14	1	15	43	20	—	—	—	—	1,843
Port Ellen	—	—	—	6	7	13	17	17	—	—	—	—	2,039
Portaskaig	—	1	—	14	1	16	29	17	—	—	—	—	2,650
Portnahaven and Port Wemyss	—	—	—	4	3	7	9	11	—	—	20	20	402
Bowmore	—	—	—	2	1	3	3	5	—	—	38	193	—
Port Charlotte	—	—	—	3	4	7	9	10	—	—	97	274	560
Bruichladdich	—	—	—	2	1	3	3	5	—	—	65	179	1,085
Loch Gruinart	—	—	—	—	—	—	—	—	—	—	12	12	—
Jura	—	—	—	6	2	8	6	12	—	—	—	—	58
Colonsay	—	—	—	2	9	11	9	13	—	—	—	—	12
Sold at Sea	—	—	—	—	—	—	—	—	2,342	2,925	—	—	—
Totals	—	38	—	73	31	142	955	‡387	38,421	40,872	23,004	43,001	13,082

‡Including 91 crofter fishermen.

Place.	Fishing Craft. 30 feet keel and upwards. Steam	Motor	Sail	Under 30 feet keel. Motor	Sail	Total. No.	Tons	Fishermen. No.	Quantity and Value of Fish Landed by British Vessels. Herrings. Cwts.	£	Other kinds (except Shell Fish). Cwts.	£	Value of Shell Fish. £
Inveraray District.													
Luing	—	—	—	12	4	16	27	30	—	—	—	—	819
Crinan	—	—	—	—	3	3	4	4	—	—	—	—	1
Tarbert	—	10	—	21	—	31	367	120	10,486	2,340	14	27	1,239
Ardrishaig	—	1	—	8	3	12	47	28	2,940	661	56	98	391
Lochgair	—	—	—	—	2	2	2	4	—	—	—	—	—
Minard	—	1	—	—	—	1	17	4	—	—	—	—	—
Inveraray	—	—	—	—	2	2	1	3	12,426	4,533	—	—	—
Cairndhu to Newton	—	—	—	—	1	1	1	2	—	—	—	—	—
Sold at Sea	—	—	—	—	—	—	—	—	32,945	9,657	—	—	—
Totals	—	12	—	41	15	68	466	195	58,797	17,191	70	125	2,450
Rothesay District.													
Rothesay	—	—	—	9	1	10	86	33	1,754	459	322	713	1,351
Port Bannatyne	—	—	—	2	—	2	11	7	—	—	—	—	—
St. Ninian's	—	—	—	—	1	1	2	1	—	—	—	—	—
Kilchattan Bay	—	1	—	—	1	2	14	5	—	—	—	—	—
Kyles of Bute	—	1	—	2	1	4	8	9	—	—	34	31	54
Toward to Holy Loch	—	—	—	3	2	5	8	10	24	10	105	169	83
Blairmore to Loch Goil	—	—	—	1	1	2	4	3	} 15	8	103	67	43
Kilcreggan to Arrochar	—	—	—	2	2	4	15	8					
Lochranza to Caticol	—	—	—	2	—	2	25	6	—	—	18	46	153
Pirnmill to Blackwater	—	1	—	1	—	2	27	9	—	—	—	—	—

Place.	Fishing Craft. 30 feet keel and upwards.			Under 30 feet keel.		Total.		Fishermen.	Quantity and Value of Fish Landed by British Vessels. Herrings.		Other kinds (except Shell Fish).		Value of Shell Fish.
	Steam	Motor	Sail	Motor	Sail	No.	Tons	No.	Cwts.	£	Cwts.	£	£
Inveraray District.													
Luing	—	—	—	17	3	20	30	17	—	—	—	—	1,019
Lochs Feochan and Melfort	—	—	—	4	1	5	14	3	—	—	—	—	—
Crinan	—	—	—	5	2	7	7	5	1,923	1,430	26	54	—
Tarbert	—	18	—	18	—	36	478	124	139,870	147,154	7,692	15,196	5,570
Ardrishaig	—	1	—	14	1	16	15	10	1,088	923	12	22	887
Lochgilphead	—	—	—	—	2	2	3	—	—	—	—	—	—
Inveraray	—	—	—	1	2	3	2	4	4,002	4,465	—	—	—
Cairndhu to Newton	—	—	—	1	1	2	3	3	—	—	—	—	—
Sold at Sea	—	—	—	—	—	—	—	—	630	780	—	—	—
Totals	—	19	—	60	12	91	587	166	147,513	154,752	7,730	15,272	7,476
Rothesay District.													
Rothesay	—	3	—	3	4	10	68	27	68	74	1,024	3,344	2,509
Port Bannatyne	—	2	—	3	4	9	52	19	—	—	—	—	—
St. Ninian's	—	—	—	—	1	1	1	1	—	—	—	—	—
Kilchattan Bay	—	1	—	—	1	2	14	—	—	—	—	—	—
Kyles of Bute	—	2	—	3	1	6	29	9	—	—	—	—	882
Toward to Holy Loch	—	1	—	4	—	5	20	9	—	—	248	499	1,276
Blairmore to Loch Goil	—	—	—	1	2	3	4	2	17	20	26	41	—
Kilcreggan to Arrochar	—	1	—	1	1	3	10	7	—	—	—	—	—

Place.	Fishing Craft.							Fishermen.	Quantity and Value of Fish Landed by British Vessels.				
	30 feet keel and upwards.			Under 30 feet keel.		Total.			Herrings.		Other kinds (except Shell Fish).		Value of Shell Fish.
	Steam	Motor	Sail	Motor	Sail	No.	Tons	No.	Cwts.	£	Cwts.	£	£
Rothesay District. (Contd.)													
Whiting Bay to Lamlash	—	—	—	—	2	2	1	3	—	—	23	48	392
Sold at Sea	—	—	—	—	—	—	—	—	340	71	—	—	—
Totals	—	3	—	22	11	36	201	94	2,133	548	605	1,074	2,076
Greenock District.													
Gareloch	—	—	—	—	—	—	—	—	—	—	—	—	91
Helensburgh	—	1	—	1	—	2	15	5	25	7	91	171	176
Glasgow	—	1	—	1	1	3	21	6	382	60	—	—	—
Port Glasgow	—	1	—	3	—	4	40	9	—	—	—	—	—
Greenock	—	3	—	2	5	10	61	19	48,944	17,251	—	—	80
Gourock	—	—	—	—	—	—	—	—	73,980	27,880	141	36	—
Wemyss Bay	—	—	—	—	—	—	—	—	—	—	33	39	43
Largs	—	—	—	2	5	7	9	14	1,092	279	283	587	80
Cumbraes	—	—	—	1	—	1	3	2	—	—	13	25	—
Fairlie	—	—	—	1	—	1	3	2	105	28	—	—	476
Saltcoats	—	—	—	5	4	9	29	19	—	—	—	—	529
Ardrossan	—	—	—	1	—	1	14	3	—	—	—	—	—
Troon	—	—	—	13	3	16	39	24	455	110	153	220	57
Totals	—	6	—	30	18	54	234	103	124,983	45,615	714	1,078	1,532
Ballantrae District.													
Ayr	—	—	—	3	—	3	6	4	139,247	40,042	31,033	33,938	20
Dunure	—	18	—	1	—	19	304	100	—	—	87	70	161
Maidens	—	9	—	7	1	17	205	56	—	—	130	195	10

Place.	Fishing Craft. 30 feet keel and upwards. Steam	Motor	Sail	Under 30 feet keel. Motor	Sail	Total. No.	Tons	Fishermen. No.	Quantity and Value of Fish Landed by British Vessels. Herrings. Cwts.	£	Other kinds (except Shell Fish). Cwts.	£	Value of Shell Fish. £
Rothesay District. (Contd.)													
Lochranza to Caticol	—	—	—	7	—	7	16	6	—	—	—	—	—
Pirnmill to Blackwater	—	—	—	1	1	2	3	5	—	—	—	—	—
Whiting Bay to Lamlash	—	—	—	3	—	3	5	6	—	—	—	—	1,544
Sold at Sea	—	—	—	—	—	—	—	—	33	635	—	—	—
Totals	—	10	—	26	15	51	222	91	618	729	1,298	3,884	6,211
Greenock District.													
Gareloch	—	—	—	—	—	—	—	—	—	—	—	—	98
Helensburgh	—	—	—	1	1	2	7	3	—	—	—	—	59
Dumbarton	—	1	—	3	—	4	46	8	—	—	—	—	—
Glasgow	—	2	—	1	—	3	24	10	—	—	—	—	—
Port Glasgow	—	—	—	3	—	3	16	3	—	—	—	—	—
Greenock	—	—	—	2	1	3	17	4	5,844	4,876	427	199	—
Wemyss Bay	—	2	—	—	—	2	23	6	—	—	—	—	134
Largs	—	1	—	3	1	5	21	3	2,755	3,341	581	1,418	15
Cumbraes	—	—	—	2	1	3	7	3	27	31	95	195	94
Portincross	—	—	—	2	—	2	4	2	—	—	—	—	—
Saltcoats	—	1	—	7	—	8	36	14	—	—	—	—	340
Irvine	—	1	—	8	—	9	63	6	—	—	2	10	—
Troon	—	1	—	12	5	18	75	28	—	—	1,450	4,134	9
Totals	—	9	—	44	9	62	339	90	8,626	8,248	2,555	5,956	749

Place.	Fishing Craft. 30 feet keel and upwards. Steam	Motor	Sail	Under 30 feet keel. Motor	Sail	Total. No.	Tons	Fishermen. No.	Quantity and Value of Fish Landed by British Vessels. Herrings. Cwts.	£	Other kinds (except Shell Fish). Cwts.	£	Value of Shell Fish. £
Ballantrae District. (Contd.)													
Girvan	—	24	—	10	—	34	443	132	3,972	1,140	687	972	1,095
Ballantrae	—	—	—	4	1	5	10	5	—	—	—	—	28
Cairnryan	—	2	—	—	—	2	23	8	—	—	—	—	—
Stranraer	—	3	—	4	3	10	63	30	1,617	402	7,863	9,883	621
Kirkcolm	—	—	—	3	2	5	6	3	—	—	2	1	76
Portpatrick	—	—	—	7	2	9	30	8	—	—	478	653	39
Port Logan	—	—	—	3	8	11	11	6	—	—	12	9	26
Drummore	—	—	—	3	9	12	15	4	—	—	543	1,023	31
Sandhead	—	—	—	3	3	6	7	6	—	—	24	38	100
Glenluce	—	—	—	1	3	4	6	2	—	—	—	—	4
Port William	—	—	—	4	10	14	18	8	—	—	274	344	328
Isle of Whithorn ...	—	1	—	7	4	12	29	7	—	—	—	—	183
Garlieston	—	—	—	3	1	4	6	6	—	—	60	185	276
Creetown	—	—	—	—	2	2	2	2	—	—	189	364	—
Kirkcudbright	—	—	—	7	1	8	18	6	—	—	55	81	571
Kippford	—	—	—	3	2	5	9	3	—	—	—	—	358
Carsethorn	—	—	—	5	—	5	14	8	—	—	89	103	218
Glencaple	—	—	—	—	—	—	—	15	—	—	337	340	—
Annan	—	—	—	22	9	31	120	27	—	—	1,644	2,280	1,513
Totals	—	57	—	100	61	218	1,345	446	144,836	41,584	43,507	50,479	5,653
Grand Totals for 1938	§748	910	8	1,561	1,840	5,067	72,467	†17,915	2,800,610	1,062,981	2,579,952	2,763,690	79,853
Grand Totals for 1937	§831	925	8	1,520	1,933	5,217	77,188	†19,364	2,140,093	962,318	2,561,564	2,459,860	92,734

§320 trawlers and 428 drifters or liners in 1938 against 346 trawlers, 485 drifters or liners in 1937.
†Including 4,067 crofter fishermen in1938 against 4,355 in 1937.

Place.	Fishing Craft. 30 feet keel and upwards. Steam	Motor	Sail	Under 30 feet keel. Motor	Sail	Total. No.	Tons	Fishermen. No.	Herrings. Cwts.	£	Other kinds (except Shell Fish). Cwts.	£	Value of Shell Fish. £
Ballantrae District.													
Ayr	—	5	—	1	—	6	181	40	121,598	129,546	34,190	92,633	303
Dunure	—	15	—	4	1	20	280	121	—	—	—	—	293
Maidens	—	11	—	6	—	17	280	94	—	—	30	158	—
Girvan	—	24	—	11	—	35	548	150	21,735	24,575	1,052	2,618	2,193
Ballantrae	—	—	—	3	—	3	10	10	490	550	37	210	156
Cairnryan	—	2	—	—	1	3	26	13	—	—	—	—	—
Stranraer	—	6	—	6	4	16	121	46	3,518	4,247	9,391	19,565	354
Kirkcolm	—	—	—	2	1	3	3	3	—	—	—	—	250
Portpatrick	—	1	—	5	1	7	41	16	20,815	24,275	5,599	11,845	—
Port Logan	—	—	—	2	2	4	3	3	—	—	—	—	—
Drummore	—	1	—	1	3	5	11	7	—	—	2,261	8,291	15
Sandhead	—	—	—	2	1	3	4	2	—	—	—	—	—
Port William	—	—	—	11	1	12	15	13	—	—	815	1,972	490
Isle of Whithorn	—	—	—	7	—	7	8	8	—	—	1,271	2,656	912
Garliestown	—	—	—	1	1	2	3	3	—	—	3,615	7,006	589
Creetown	—	—	—	2	2	4	8	4	—	—	38	107	—
Kirkcudbright	—	—	—	8	1	9	14	13	—	—	—	—	876
Kippford	—	—	—	6	—	6	14	8	—	—	—	—	459
Carsethorn	—	—	—	2	—	2	4	5	—	—	189	598	2,160
Glencaple	—	—	—	—	—	—	—	10	—	—	—	—	—
Annan	—	—	—	22	2	24	105	34	—	—	1,210	3,940	13,000
Totals	—	65	—	102	21	188	1,679	603	168,156	183,193	59,698	151,599	22,050
Grand Totals for 1948	§487	1,079	4	2,543	1,184	5,297	66,634	†17,228	2,913,163	3,078,792	3,493,463	8,529,592	430,066
Grand Totals for 1947	§489	972	3	2,338	1,335	5,137	62,528	†16,326	2,287,028	2,398,377	3,694,525	8,109,258	388,834

*237 trawlers and 250 drifters or liners in 1948 against 234 trawlers, 255 drifters or liners in 1947.
†Including 3,733 crofter fishermen in 1948 against 3,354 in 1947.

(2)

BIBLIOGRAPHY

It would take up too much space to give a complete bibliography of Scottish fisheries. Reference should be made to *A Contribution to the Bibliography of Scottish Topography* by Sir Arthur Mitchell, K.C.B., F.R.S.G.S. 2 Vols. Edinburgh, 1917. Here is a list of the more important sources of reference.

Reports of Royal Commissions and Committees of Inquiry, 1785-1932.
Fishery Board for Scotland: Annual Reports and Statistics, 1887-1938.
Publications of the Fishery Board for Scotland: 1922-1928.
Scottish Home Department: *Report on the Fisheries of Scotland*, 1939-1948.
Fishing Industry, Report of Committee of Economic Advisory Council, 1932.
Herring Industry, 1st Report of Sea-Fish Commission for the U.K., 1934.
White Fish Industry, 2nd Report of Sea-Fish Commission for the U.K., 1936.
The Highlands and Islands of Scotland (Scottish Economic Committee Publication, 1938).

Kyle, H. M. *Die Seefischerei von Grossbritannien und Irland (Handbuch die Seefischerei Nordeuropas*. Band VI.) Stuttgart, 1929. The only fairly recent comprehensive treatise on Scottish fisheries.
Holdsworth, E. W. H. *Deep Sea Fishing and Fishing Boats*. London, 1874
Graham, Michael. *The Fish Gate*. London, 1943.
Thomson, James. *The Value and Importance of the Scottish Fisheries*. London, 1849.
Knox, John. *A View of the British Empire—more especially Scotland*. Edinburgh, 1789.
M'Culloch, L. *Observations on the Herring Fisheries upon the North and East Coasts of Scotland*. 2 parts. 1788-90. London.
Jenkins, J. T. *The Sea Fisheries*. London, 1920.
The Herring & the Herring Fisheries. London, 1927.
Pitcairn, George. *A Prospective View of the Scots Fisheries*. Edinburgh, 1788.
Williams, J. *On Promoting and Improving the Fisheries upon the Coasts of the Highlands and Islands*. (Trans. Highland Society. I. Edinburgh, 1799.)
Sinclair, Sir John. *Statistical Account of Scotland*. 22 vols. 1791-1795.
New Statistical Account of Scotland. 15 vols. 1845.
Anson, Peter F. *Fishing Boats and Fisher Folk on the East Coast of Scotland*. London, 1930.
Fishermen and Fishing Ways. London, 1932.
The Scottish Fisheries—are they doomed? Edinburgh, 1938.
British Sea Fishermen (Britain in Pictures). London, 1944.

(2) *East Coast*

Hutcheson, G. *Days of Yore, or Buckie Past and Present*. Banff, 1887.
Buchan, B. *Annals of Peterhead*. Peterhead, 1819.
Cranna, J. *Fraserburgh, Past and Present*. Aberdeen, 1914.
Clark, V. E. *The Port of Aberdeen*. Aberdeen, 1921.
Leatham, James. *Fisherfolk of the North East*. Turriff, 1932.
Bruce, W. *The Nor'-East*. Aberdeen, 1921.
McGibbon, R. *The Fisher Folk of Buchan*. London, n.d.
Farnie, H. *Handbook of the Fifeshire Coast*. Cupar, 1860.
Gourlay, G. *Memorials of Cellardyke: or Fisher Life*. Cupar, 1879.
Crupples, Mrs. *Newhaven: its Origins and History*. Edinburgh, 1888.
Russell, J. *The Story of Leith*. London, 1922.

McInver, D. *An Old Time Fishing Ground: Eyemouth.* Greenock, 1906.

(3) *Orkney and Shetland.*

Tudor, John R. *The Orkneys and Shetland.* London, 1883.

(There are innumerable books on these islands mentioning the fisheries, but Tudor's work remains the most authoritative.)

(4) *West Coast*

Martin, M. *Description of the Western Islands of Scotland.* London, 1705. (Reprinted, Glasgow, 1884).

MacCulloch, J. *Description of the Western Islands.* 3 vols. Edinburgh 1824.

Minutes of Evidence of the Crofter Commission. Edinburgh, 1884.

Campbell, D. *Historical Sketches of the Town and Harbours of Greenock.* 2 vols. Glasgow, 1879-81.

Smith, Anderson. *Lewisiana, or Life in the Outer Hebrides.* London, 1875.

Goodrich-Freer, A. *The Outer Isles.* London, 1902.

Buchanan, Donald. *Reflections of the Isle of Barra.* London, 1943.

Campbell, John L. *The Book of Barra.* London, 1936.

Beaton, A. J. *The Island of Lewis and its Fishermen-Crofters.* London, 1878.

Buchanan, R. *The Hebrid Isles.* London, 1883.

Mitchison, N., and *Men and Herring.* 1949.

Macintosh, D.

(5) *Fiction*

Gunn, Neil M. *The Grey Coast.* London 1926.
Hidden Doors. London, 1929.
Morning Tide. London, 1931.
The Silver Darlings. London, 1941.

Macdonald, G. *The Marquis of Lossie.*

Scott, Sir Walter. *The Antiquary* (references to Auchmithie).

Reade, Charles. *Christie Johnstone* (Newhaven).

(3)

DETAILS OF OLD TYPES OF SCOTTISH FISHING VESSELS*

(I) SHETLAND SIXERN

Type. Double-ended. *District.* Whole of Shetland.
Stem. Curved.
Stern. Curved.
L.O.A. 26ft. to 32ft. Keel 18ft. to 27ft.
Beam. 8ft. to 10ft.
Depth in hold. 24in. to 28in.
Tonnage. 3 to 7 tons (approx.)
Clinker built.
Undecked.
Paintwork. Nearly all tarred.
Fishing numbers. Plain: none until recent times.
Bottom. Tarred.
Rig. One square sail, tack on forequarter, with bowline. In Whalsay sails always white first season, then barked.
No. of masts. One.
Details. Later boats fitted with a pump. Some boats could pull 8 oars.
Class of fishing employed in. White fishing. A very few at herring down to late 1890's.
Period of use. Very early times down to late 'nineties.

(II) SHETLAND FOURAREEN

Type. Double-ended. *District.* Whole of Shetland.
Stem. Curved.
Stern. Curved.
L.O.A. Large haddock boats (say) 22ft. Keel 16ft. Ordinary boat for pulling and sailing (say) 16ft. Keel 10ft. or 11ft. "Whillie" for pulling. 12ft. or 13ft. Keel 8ft. or 9ft.
Beam. According to proportions of sixern.
Draught. According to proportions of sixern.
Depth in hold. According to proportions of sixern. A "Whillie" is very shallow.
Tonnage. Uncertain.
Clinker built.
Undecked.
Paintwork. Many gaily painted. Usually topsides and bottoms. No cutwaters. Painted grey inside very often.
Fishing numbers. Plain. None until recent times.
Bottom. Painted. White (usually). Black or copper antifouling.
Rig. One square sail (vide sixern) but more often jib and standing lug—with or without boom.
No. of masts. One.
Details. Some haddock boats could pull 6 oars.
Class of fishing employed in. Now mostly handlines. Sometimes long lines.
Period of use. To present day.

(III) SHETLAND DANDY-RIGGED HERRING BOAT.

Type. Double-ended fifie. elliptic: Zulu.
Stem. Slight rake.
Stern. Rakes various: in many cases were bought second-hand.

---

*These notes have been compiled by R. Stuart Bruce of Whalsay, Shetland.

Depth in hold. 5½ft. to 9ft.
Tonnage. 25 to 70 and even more.
Almost invariably carvel. A few early boats, c. 1890, clincher.
Decked or undecked. Decked: low bulwarks, about 1ft. or less.
Paintwork. See III. Cutters, decks black.
Fishing numbers. See III. Name usually on both bows, and on port side right aft. Creek name on starboard side aft. This applies to the old cutters.
Rig. Dandy with boom to mainsail (5 reefs). (2 reefs in staysail), and lug mizzen sheeted to boomkin. Often jib headed riding mizzen.
No. of masts. Two. Pole main mast.
Details. Wheel steering in later boats, and steam capstans. "Iron man" in early boats.
Class of fishing employed in. Earlier boats went to spring white fishing, then herring. Some went to Yarmouth and Lowestoft winter herring fishing.
Period of use. From about 1882 to present day.

Details of an early dandy fifie are as follows: RESEARCH. L.K.828, of Whalsay. Builders, Carnegie and Matthew, Peterhead. Keel laid March, 1902, and boat launched May, 1902. L.O.A. 65ft. 5ins. Keel 60ft. Beam 20ft. 9ins. from outside gunwale to outside gunwale. Depth in hold 8ft. 5ins. 52 tons. Steam capstan. Sail area: mainsail, 226 sq. yds. Lug-mizzen. 96 sq. yds. Foresail 60 sq. yds. Big jib 86 sq. yds. 2nd jib, 50 sq. yds. 3rd jib, 25 sq. yds. Area of topsail and jib-headed riding mizzen not given. (Letter to R. Stuart Bruce from Magnus Polson, the skipper of the boat, dated December 1901.) This boat was at the herring fishing in 1933.

Many Zulu dandies were of course much larger than this boat. Some about 80ft. cut down rig, with motors, are owned in Shetland, and one *sailing* Zulu belongs to Whalsay at the present day, the *Gracie Brown*, L.K. 1075, a carvel boat of 74ft. 5ins. L.O.A. Many ketch and dandy-rigged boats were owned in Shetland, with elliptic sterns, mostly built in Scotland for Shetland owners. Some converted sail boats have red decks and bulwarks.

(IV) EARLY HALF-DECKED SHETLAND HERRING BOATS

C. 1820 to 1840. Many of these boats, which seem nearly all to have been fifie built, were luggers, some cutters, and some with a single mast, with stay foresail and sprit mainsail without a boom, and sometimes a bowsprit and jib. Very little seems to be known of these boats. They seem to have been about 30ft. keel.

After these boats, say 1840 to c. 1876, came a number of wholly decked boats, mostly built at Wick. With very large hatches and waterways, some two-masted luggers and others cutter-rigged. These boats were very broad and were bluff in the bows, and ran to about 38ft. of keel.

The late seventies saw the beginning of the true decked herring boat in Shetland: luggers or cutters.

The main-mast lowers into a metal crutch, served with rope, on the starboard side of the mizzen mast. This is a common shape.

(V) ORKNEY BOATS

(a) North Isles Boat

Type. Double-ended. *District:* north part of Orkney.
Stem. Raked. Keel 11ft. to 20ft.
Stern. Raked.
Length over all. 15ft. to 20ft. keel; on keel 14ft.; breadth 7.9ft.; depth amidships 2.8ft.
Clinker built. Undecked.
Paintwork. White topsides in modern times. Tarred formerly.
Bottom. Usually black or green. Tarred formerly.
Rig. Two standing lugs, jib and bowsprit, main lug usually with boom.

No. of masts. Two
Class of fishing employed in: white and herring.
In Shetland, these boats are called *FLATCHIES.*

(b) South Isles Boat

Type. Double-ended. *District:* south part of Orkney.
Stem. As in No. 1.
Stern. As in No. 1.
Length over all. As in No. 1.
Beam and Draught. As in No. 1.
Depth of hold. As in No. 1.
Tonnage. As in No. 1.
Clinker built.
Undecked.
Paintwork. As in No. 1.
Fishing numbers. As in No. 1.
Bottom. As in No. 1.
Rig. Two sprit-sails, jib and bowsprit, or formerly without jib.
No. of masts. Two.
Class of fishing employed in. Same as North Isle Boats.

For herring boats, see notes on Shetland, which apply well to Orkney. Orkney boats far fewer in number always, and therefore not the same diversity of types and rigs.

(VI) SCOTTISH HERRING BOATS

(a) Two-masted Skaffie

Type. Curved stem, raking sternpost. *Districts.* INS., BF., WK. Double ended.
Length O.A. 41ft. Keel 32ft. 2in.
Beam. 13ft.
Draught. 4ft. 9in.
Tonnage. 3.
Clinker built. Decked.
Paintwork. Early boats dark varnished topsides, with blue, white or green steerstrake, blue or white rail. Later boats white cutwaters, some being painted as the Shetland cutter boats.
Fishing numbers. Plain.
Bottom. Green or red antifouling or black.
Rig. Two masts, two lugs, fore lug dipped, fore mast lowered into a crutch. A spar-bowling used for big lug down to 1880. A jib sometimes set. No mizzen staysail
Motors fitted to a few remaining skaffies.
Other details. Iron wife and iron man for hauling nets, never steam capstan.
Class of fishing employed in. White fishing and herring fishing.

(b) Fifie

Type. Double ended.
Stem. Slight rake or nearly vertical.
Stern. Rake of 3ft. to 5ft.
Length O.A. Large up to 73ft. Keel 68ft.
Small up to 50ft. Keel 46ft.
Beam. Large to 21ft.
Depth in hold. Large to 9ft.
Tonnage. From 18 to 60, gross.
Old, clinker built; Modern, carvel. Open, half-decked or decked.
Paintwork. Early boats tarred. Modern boats vide paint of Shetland boats.
Fishing numbers. Early, plain. Modern, picked out in colours, *i.e.* white with blue shading, etc.
Bottom. Early, tarred. Modern, vide Shetland boats.
Rig. See Skaffie, but spar bowlines may not have been used.
Other details. Iron "wife": iron "man": then steam capstans. Impossible to hoist large modern sails or haul nets without steam.
Class of fishing. Early Fifies; white fish and herring. Modern, herring.

(c) Zulu

Type. Double ended.
Stem. Rake of about 1ft.
Stern. Rake of 45°.
L.O.A. Largest boats over 84ft. Keel 60ft.—65ft.
Beam. Up to 22ft.—21ft.
Depth in hold. To 9ft. or more.
Tonnage. Over 60 gross.
A few clinker, rest carvel built. Decked.
Paintwork. See modern Shetland boats.
Fishing numbers. Early, plain. Modern, see "Fifie."
Bottom. Copper, red or green antifouling, or black.
Rig. Two masts, dipping fore lug (7 reefs) and standing mizzen (2 or 3 reefs). A jib sometimes used when making a passage. No mizzen staysail.
Motor. Motors fitted to nearly all remaining Zulus.
Other details. See "Fifie."
Employed in white and herring fishing.

Among the largest Zulus were the *Spikenard, Cynosure, Laverock.* and *Lord Kitchener* (all Buckie District). Their average sizes were: L.O.A. 84 feet; keel 59 feet, beam 20 feet 7 inches; depth in hold, 11 feet.

(d) Baldie

Type. Double ended.
Stem. Slight rake or vertical.
Stern. Rake of 1ft. to 2ft.
L.O.A. 24ft. up to 36ft. Keel 21ft. to 32ft.
Beam. 8ft. 2ins.
Depth in hold. 3ft. 7ins.
Early, clinker; modern, carvel built. Decked with large hatch.
Paintwork. See modern Shetland boats. Early boats were often tarred.
Fishing numbers. See "Fifie."
Bottom. Black, green, red or copper paint.
Rig. Two masts. Dipping forelug. Often with jib, and standing mizzen.
Other details. See "Fifie," but never steam capstan.
Class of fishing employed in. White fishing and herring.

Details of the various types of undecked fishing vessels in use for the herring fishing off the coast of Scotland previous to 1855 From Captain Swinburne's *Rig of Fishing Boats on the Coast of Scotland* (1883).

(1) *Moray Firth "South" built,* i.e. *from Banff to Portmahomack.* "Skaffie" type, with round stem and very raked stern. Typical example of Buckie boat, 1850. Length 41 feet; keel 32 feet 2 inches; breadth 13 feet, depth 4 feet 9 inches; displacement 3 tons; cost £60; crew, 5 men; rig, 2 lug-sails and jib; clinker built.

(2) *Banff to Eyemouth* and *north-west side of Moray Firth from Portmahomack to Wick.* "Fifie" type, round stem and slightly rounded stern with slight rake.

(a) *Aberdeen boat.* Length 39 feet; keel 31 feet 8 inches; breadth 12 feet 6 inches; depth 4 feet 3 inches; displacement 4.8 tons; cost £65; crew 5 men; rig, 2 lug-sails; clinker built.

(b) *Peterhead boat.* Length 37 feet 6 inches; breadth 13 feet 6 inches; depth 4 feet 9 inches; displacement 5 tons; cost £68; crew 5 men; rig, 2 lug-sails; clinker built.

(c) *Fraserburgh boat.* Length 36 feet; breadth 13 feet 6 inches; depth, 4 feet 6 inches; displacement, 2.6 tons; crew 5 men; rig, 2 lug-sails; clinker built.

(d) *Wick boat.* Length 34 feet 6 inches; breadth 13 feet; depth 4 feet 9 inches; displacement 4 tons; cost £64; crew 5 men; rig, 2 lug-sails; clinker built.

INDEX

Aberdeen, 1, 23, 49, 50, 53, 54, 70, 73, 74, 75, 76, 77, 84, 93, 104, 111.
Achastle, 57.
Annan, 69, 108.
Anstruther, 52, 77, 84, 93, 98.
Arbroath, 53, 93.
Ardchattan Priory, 1.
Ardersier, 17, 24 32.
Auchmithie, 53.
Auckingill, 58.
Avoch, 24, 57.
Ayr, 68, 70, 76.
Anderson, Rev. A., 24.

Balintore, 57.
Ballantrae, 68, 93, 94, 108.
Banff, 8, 39, 55, 84, 93, 111.
Barents Sea, 72.
Barra, Isle of, 65, 66, 82, 48.
Bear Island, 72.
Beauly Priory, 1.
Bernera, 97.
Berwick, 1.
Black Isle, 48.
Boddam, 30, 35, 54.
Bremen, 2.
Bressay 61.
Broadsea, 30.
Broughty Ferry, 53.
Buckhaven, 8, 31, 52, 54.
Buckie, 15, 20, 24, 32, 34, 38, 39, 50, 56, 81, 84, 93, 111.
Buckpool, 56.
Buchan, 42, 48.
Buchanhaven, 54.
Burghead 8, 57.
Burnmouth, 52.
Burntisland, 8, 52.
Bute, Isle of, 3, 68.
Brand, John (1701), 61.
Bertram, James, 17, 19, 21, 24.

Cairnbulg, 54.
Caithness, 4.
Campbeltown, 50 67, 93, 94.
Canna, 48, 64.
Carradale, 67.
Castlebay, 65, 80, 81.
Cellardyke, 8, 16, 52.
Clyde, Firth of, 2, 3, 7, 67, 68.
Coll 64.
Cockenzie, 52.
Collieston, 31, 32, 54.
Cove, 53.
Crail, 53.
Cromarty, 57.
Crovie, 31, 33, 38, 39, 55.
Cullen, 8, 37, 56.
Cullivoe, 62.
Campbell, Rev. J. G., 41.
Campbell, William, 105.
Charles I, 2.
Charles II, 3.

Denmark, 10.
Donegal, 26.
Downies, 55.
Dumbarton, 3.
Dunbar 8, 9, 23, 42, 52.
Dundee, 53, 70, 73.
Dunure, 68, 108.
Dysart, 52.
Defoe, Daniel, 69.
Donaldson, Rev. G., 20.

East and West Haven, 53.
Eigg, 48, 64.
Eriskay, 48, 66.
Eyemouth 8, 16, 17, 48, 52, 84, 93, 98.

Fair Isle, 102.
Faroes, 61, 72, 75.
Ferryden, 53.
Fetlar, 60.
Findhorn, 57, 93.
Findochty, 38, 56.
Fisherrow, 22, 23, 52.
Footdee, 14, 17 24, 54.
Forse, 57.
Fort William (District of), 64, 93, 94, 97.
Foula, 61.
Fraserburgh, 8, 30, 42, 54, 65, 80, 81, 84, 93, 98, 104, 111.
Freswick, 58.
Farnie, Henry, 16.
Fife, Earl of, 55.

Gairloch, 63.
Gardenstown, 31, 33, 55.
Gigha, 67.
Girvan, 68.
Glasgow, 1, 3, 68.
Glenluce, 69.
Glenelg, 63.
Gourdon, 53.
Gourock, 68.
Granton, 52, 70, 73, 76.
Grimsby, 80, 103.
Greenock 3, 67, 68, 93.
George I, 1.
George IV, 21.
Graham Michael, 86.
Graham, H. G., 28.
Gregor, Rev. W., 32.
George, Rev. W., 38.

Hamburg, 2.
Hartlepool, 50.
Hebrides, 2, 3, 7, 26, 43, 64-67, 97, 107.
Helmsdale, 8, 57, 93.
Hilton, 57.
Holland, 2, 3.
Hopeman, 57.
Hardy, A. C., 87.

Inverallochy, 54.
Inverary, 93.
Inverness, 57.
Islay, 67.
Isle, Maryin 63.
Isle of Whithorn, 69.

Johnshaven, 53.
Jura, 67.
James III, 1, 3.
James IV, 2.
James V. 2.
James VI, 2.
Jenkins, Dr W. T., 7.

Keiss, 58.
Kinghorn, 52.
Kirkcaldy, 52.
Kirkwall, 50, 59.
Kyle of Lochalsh, 64.
Knox, John (1789), 5, 6, 23.

Largo, 52.
Latheronwheel, 46, 57.
Leith, 52, 70, 73, 93, 98.
Lerwick, 26, 49, 50, 61, 62, 80, 82, 111.
Levenwick, 62.
Leverburgh, 66.
Lewis, 2, 42.
Lismore, 64.
Loch Boisdale, 65.
Loch Carron, 97.
Loch Fyne, 8, 67, 80, 107, 108.
Lochinver, 64.
Loch Ryan, 68, 98.
Lossiemouth, 8, 56, 93, 105, 110, 111.
Lowestoft, 25, 26, 50, 80, 82.
Lybster, 8, 57, 93.
Leverhulme, Lord, 66.

Macduff, 8, 31, 55, 93, 106, 110, 111.
Maidens, 68, 108.
Mallaig, 64, 77, 80.
Mid Yell, 62.
Minch, The, 66, 67.
Montrose, 53, 93, 98.
Moray Firth, 3, 15, 37, 47, 55-57, 73, 75, 97, 103, 104, 105, 106.
Muchalls, 53.
Mull, 64.
Methuen, James, 65.
Miller, Hugh, 41.

Nairn, 15, 38, 39, 57.
Newburgh, 54.
Newhaven, 19, 21-23, 31, 52.
North Berwick, 52.
North Shields, 80.
Norway, 9, 10, 100.

Oban, 64, 76, 77.
Orkneys, 59-60, 97, 100, 102, 103, 104.

Pennan, 55.
Peterhead, 8, 15, 49, 50, 54, 76, 80, 81, 93, 104, 111.
Pittenweem, 52.
Pittulie, 55.
Pluscarden Priory, 1.
Port Erroll, 54.
Portessie, 38, 39, 40, 56.
Port Gordon, 56.
Portknockie, 39, 56.
Portlethen, 53.
Port Logan, 68.
Portmahomack, 38, 57.
Port Patrick, 68, 108.
Port Seton, 52.
Portsoy, 8, 56, 103.
Port William, 69.

Rockall, 61.
Rosehearty, 31, 55.
Rothesay, 68, 93.
Rum, 64.

St. Andrews, 1, 53.
St. Combs, 34, 54.
St. Monans, 52, 53, 111.
Salen, 64.
Saltcoats, 68
Sandend, 56.
Sandhaven, 55, 111.
Sandhead, 68
Scalloway, 62.
Scarborough, 80.
Shetland, 2, 3, 6, 59-62, 81, 84, 93, 94, 100-103, 104.
Skateraw, 53.
Skerries, 60, 62.
Skye, 63.
Solway Firth, 69.
South Ronaldsay, 59.
Staxigoe, 58.
Stockinish, 97.
Stonehaven, 42, 53, 93.
Stranraer, 68, 77, 80.
Stromness, 50, 59
Stronsay, 50, 59, 60, 80.
Sweden, 10.
Scott, Sir Walter, 41, 53.
Smith, Adam (1776), 7.
Smith, John (1661), 61.

Tanera, Island, 63.
Thurso, 63.
Tiree, 41, 64.
Tobermory, 4, 64.
Tongue, 63.
Torry, 54.
Thomson, James, 12.
Turner, James, 46, 47.
Troup, Jock, 47.

Uist, North, 44.
Uist, South 5, 48.
Ullapool, 4, 63, 64.

Vatersay, 66.

Westray, 108.
West Wemyss, 52.
Whalsay, 62.
Whinnyfold, 54.
Whitby, 80.
Wick, 4, 17, 49, 57, 58, 80, 82, 93, 98, 104.
Warrington Smyth, Lt.-Com. H., 106.

Yarmouth, Great, 25, 26, 50, 80, 82.

Shetland, 60, 100-102;
Sixern, 101; Fourareen, 101; Fair Isle Skiff, 102; Deep Sea Smack, 103; Ness Yole 102.

Orkney; North Isles (Westray) Yole, 102; South Isles Boat, 102, 103.
"Skaffie," 103, 104.
"Fifie," 104, 105.
"Baldie," 105.
"Zulu," 105-106.
Stornoway Yawl, 107.
Loch Fyne Nabby, 108.
Dunure and Maidens Skiffs. 108.
Portpatrick line boat, 108.
Stranraer Yawl, 108.
Manx built boats, 108.
Annan boats, 109.
Steam drifters and trawlers, 73, 74, 75, 83, 84, 109.
Motor vessels, 90, 110-111.

Bounty System, 4, 5, 6, 7.
Boats, 8.
British Sailors' Society, 50.
British Fisheries Society (1786), 4, 5.
Clothes (Fishermen's), 16-19.
Cod fisheries, 60, 61.
Crabs, 97, 98.
Crofter-fishermen, 63, 91, 95, 96, 97
Drift-net fishing, 77-90.
Fishery Board for Scotland, 8, 9.
Fish-wives, 20-24.
Great-lining, 76-77.
Herring Industry Board, 11, 86, 87
Herring-fisheries, 1, 2, 3, 7, 8, 52, 53, 54, 55, b56, 56, 59, 61-62, 64-66, 67-68, 77-90.
Houses, Fishermen's, 13-15.
Inshore fisheries (Seine-net and Lines), 90-97; East Coast, 92-95; North and West Coast, 95-97.
Line fishing, 13, 21, 25, 64, 91, 76, 77.
Lobster fisheries, 64, 97-98.
Mission to Deep Sea Fishermen, Royal National, 49, 50.
Mission to the Fisherfolk, 50.
Parliamentary Reports, 6-11.
Religion and Superstitions of fisherfolk, 28-51.
Ring-net fishing, 67, 68, 80.
Royal Fishing Companies, 2, 3.
Salmon Fisheries, 1, 53, 54, 69, 98, 99.
Sea Fish Commission, 84.
Seine-net (Danish), 54, 55, 56, 57, 92-95.
Shell Fisheries, 53, 97-98.
Superstitions, 28-45.
Birth, 28; Childhood, 29; Marriage, 29-34; Illfitted persons, 34-35; Boats, 35, 36, 37, 39; Animals, 36, 43; Names, 37, 38, 41; Death, 38, 39, 41, 43, 44; Tides, 40; the Sea, 40, 41; Shetland, 41; Highlands, 40, 41, 44, 45; "Sea Trows," 41; Mermaids, 41, 42; Fish, 42, 43; Sunday 42; Ministers, 41.
Trawling, 52, 53, 54, 70-76.
Whaling, 54, 59.
Women and girls employed in industry, 24-27.